THE UNFOLDING KINGDOM

The Unfolding Kingdom

MICHAEL LAWSON

KINGSWAY PUBLICATIONS

EASTBOURNE

ISBN 0 86065 425 7

Unless otherwise indicated biblical quotations are from
the Revised Standard Version, copyrighted 1946, 1952,
© 1971, 1973 by the Division of Christian Education of the
National Council of Churches of
Christ in the USA

NIV = Holy Bible: New International Version
© International Bible Society 1973, 1978, 1984

Front cover design by Vic Mitchell

Printed in Great Britain for
KINGSWAY PUBLICATIONS LTD
Lottbridge Drove, Eastbourne, E. Sussex BN23 6NT by
Richard Clay Ltd, Bungay, Suffolk.
Typeset by CST, Eastbourne, E. Sussex.

Contents

Life is a process and an unfolding.
                    —Lydgate in George Eliot,
                    Middlemarch (1871-72)

Foreword

Becoming a bishop is quite a shock to one's being—as one realizes how little of a bishop's life one has understood or known about before. Of course, bishops are 'there'—they appear at various events and are explained or criticized and an enormous amount is expected of them. As a bishop oneself, or as a member of a bishop's family, the role takes on an entirely new perspective. It becomes real, personal and warmly understandable.

The kingdom is like that. Everybody knows it is 'there' in Scripture, yet understanding it or knowing about it often seems remote. All sorts of people refer to 'the kingdom', explain it and seem to expect an enormous amount from it. Michael Lawson alters our entire perspective. He sets us within the kingdom family and succeeds in making the idea of the kingdom real, personal and warmly understandable. Indeed his book not only incorporates us in the kingdom, but involves us as well, filling out the whole privilege, responsibility, adventure and experience of belonging to the King of kings and his kingdom. He does this in a down-to-earth style that is illuminated by many homely day-to-day illustrations.

Once when I was at All Souls, Langham Place as a Rector, a Ghanaian Christian told us how when he first came to the church he kept hearing about 'the church family'. He said that he kept looking for this family and then gradually realized not only what was meant by it, but that he could be part of it. It had come to mean so much to him. Michael Lawson's richly woven tapestry of writing not only shows us what is meant by the kingdom but warmly encourages us as part of it.

May the kingdom come to mean so much more to all who read this book.

MICHAEL A. BAUGHEN
Bishop of Chester

Introduction

Down to earth

The kingdom of God has always been a talking point. What is it? When will it come? How will life change? These pressing and essential questions concerning the kingdom of God were as hotly debated among Jews at the beginning of the first century A.D. as they are among Christians today—in fact, far more so. When Jesus announced the imminence of the kingdom in his first major public statement, 'The time has come. The kingdom of God is near. Repent and believe the good news!' (Mk 1:15 NIV), he sent ripples of Messiah fever and kingdom speculation pulsating through the entire land of Palestine. Kingdom talk was upon everybody's lips; imaginations were fired and political hopes kindled. In consequence, Jesus found himself face to face with ideas and claims about the kingdom which were often as wild and extravagant as they were filled with enthusiasm for God and his purposes. Against this background, Jesus proclaimed that supreme purpose— to re-establish God's rule in the lives of men and women everywhere, and bring heaven down to earth.

Kingdom concerns

Jesus' kingdom is far more radical than the radicals could ever dream. Though the good news of the kingdom of God makes its clear appearance in the first three gospels, providing the major burden of the teaching of Jesus, it is in no sense *new* news. The theme of the kingdom of God unfolds right from the *beginning* of the Bible, from the covenant God made with Abraham onwards. Jesus did not inaugurate something new. The kingdom of God is the master plan to reunite heaven and earth, to usher in to individual lives, and human society as a whole, the rule and direction of the living God as an actual reality for everyday life and experience. Jesus came to fulfil what had been promised for many hundreds of years, and in him the purpose of history finds its climax.

Jesus' strategy was to spend much of his ministry correcting wrong ideas about the kingdom and its Messiah, misplaced ideas which had emerged during the period between the Testaments. By drawing on the rich heritage of God's teaching already revealed in the Old Testament, he aimed to clarify truth and revivify expectation.

Master plan

Our situation is the same today. We cannot understand the kingdom of God rightly unless we immerse ourselves in the Old Testament background which formed the backdrop and major content of all Jesus' teaching; equally we need to inform ourselves as to the kind of controversies to which Jesus was responding as he taught about the kingdom in New Testament times.

The kingdom of God was not dreamt up for the sake of the New Testament. Its unfolding nature was carefully planned and prepared by God. The kingdom is dynamic; each stage of its reality has only been unveiled at God's chosen moments in salvation-history. Indeed, it is still unfolding today.

Jesus makes us live with a paradox. The kingdom has arrived—in him—but still the best is yet to come. His passionate concern now is the same as it was for his disciples: kingdom people must learn to live lives fit for a King's rule. Privileges and responsibilities belong together. Radical discipleship, signs and wonders, social responsibility, personal spirituality—all are subservient to the grand design. The Lord of history, who is the Lord of glory, wants a people for himself to be agents of his blessing to the whole earth. This is the purpose of the unfolding kingdom. By it, the future of the whole world is assured, and God's master plan will finally come to completion. In that day it will finally be said in triumph: 'The kingdom of the world has become the kingdom of our Lord and of his Christ, and he will reign for ever and ever' (Rev 11:15 NIV).

We face the same questions in our time as did the Jews of the first century. It is natural we should long to know the nature of the kingdom, the timing of its appearance and the extent of its impact upon our lives. But we must not exclude what was for Jesus the final and most lastingly important question when contemplating the kingdom of God. If it is a fact that God is coming to rule—if he *is* bringing in his kingdom—how should we ourselves live in the light of that reality?

I

The God Who Reigns

There have always been large numbers of people who find it either inexplicable or offensive to believe in a God who reigns. The idea that God has the ability to have some kind of guiding, controlling or even overruling hand in human affairs, is viewed uncomfortably by many; they see it as a loathsome violation of freedom of choice and man's right to self-determination.

Over just this issue, Moses came into conflict with Egypt's Pharaoh, Rameses II, Elijah confronted the prophets of Baal on Mount Carmel and the apostle Paul argued with the Stoic and Epicurean philosophers at the Areopagus in first-century Athens. Today, in our largely rationalist Western culture, perhaps we are not so surprised that the assertion of God's sovereign power, his reign, often meets with similar bemused mystification or outright rejection. Yet the reign of God is a fundamental biblical truth. The offence it at times elicits goes far deeper than mere philosophical incomprehension. Such a resistance has as much to do with deeper questions of individual morality and personal response to God as with basic intellectual understanding.

Concept or co-operation?

That God desires a guiding part in our affairs is not so much a difficulty for conceptual understanding as it is a challenge to our own selves and the way we live our lives. Philosophical complexities come in a slow second to the moral ambiguities of our human nature. In the widest sense this claim to sovereignty is a direct challenge to our moral outlook: our lifestyles, concerns and priorities. Put at its very simplest it is a question of who does reign, who rules, who runs the show. It is a common experience that when we first discover that God desires a controlling and decisive part in our lives, the defences fairly quickly go up. It is part of our fallen condition to be resistant to the purposes and direction of God. Fallen humanity instinctively aims to go it alone.

The kingdom of God, then, is not so much a concept as a co-operation; not so much an idea to be explored as a relationship to be developed. God wants to co-operate with us, and us to co-operate with him, in a partnership. But it will be a partnership where he takes the initiative and where we must be prepared to open up our lives to him. This is partly what is meant in biblical terms by the reign or sovereignty of God—what the New Testament describes as the lordship of Christ. Under that sovereign lordship, no longer do we go it alone, we co-operate with the divine King himself—the God who reigns—who has great plans for us, for the church and for the world.

So when we start to think about the kingdom of God, this is where we must begin. The biblical metaphor is clear: every kingdom has a king, and every king reigns. To understand the kingdom biblically, we must therefore ask the initial question, What does it *mean* when we speak of *the God who reigns*? If this is the God whose kingdom it is, we need first to know something about *him*, in his character and his sovereign power, if he is going to have a real part to play in our lives.

History speaks today

The Bible is a historical book. That is far from implying that it is in any sense irrelevant because it was written a long time ago. By contrast, the historical nature of the Bible lies not only in *real* events which took place at a specific time and place, but also in the fact that God often taught his people about himself and his concerns for them in the light of those historical situations. As the people lived through an event with God, so their Lord would teach them about himself in relation to that specific happening. This is just one facet of the rich educative process the Lord uses throughout the Bible to teach his people about his nature, ways and will.

From the very beginning of the Old Testament it is clear that those events would often be painful movements in the history of God's people. The biblical writers themselves remind us that when we find ourselves up against it, whether in practical, personal or emotional difficulty, the great biblical affirmations about God's control, his power and goodness are significantly often made against this background of pain and suffering. What we are dealing with is not a book of philosophy or poetry sadly out of touch with the realities of everyday life, but a book which teaches us of a living experience of a real God who moves and is in all kinds of situations past and present. In a very precise sense, therefore, history speaks today.

The prophets clearly illustrate how God speaks into painful situations; their messages often were given during times of national bewilderment and turmoil. It was into one such situation that the prophet Isaiah was called to be God's spokesman. And in the confident yet reassuring words of chapter 40 of his prophecy, some of the most remarkable affirmations in the whole Bible concerning the sovereignty of God, *the God who reigns*, are made. They form one of the most comprehensive pictures of God's sovereignty in the entire Old Testament.

Both the background and details of Isaiah 40 teach us

much about the issues raised by the impressive-sounding assertion that the God of Israel is a God who is King and who reigns as the sovereign Lord over all things.

Is God in control?

In the ancient world, two of the major superpowers of Isaiah's time were Assyria and Babylon. By contrast, Israel was quite a small and relatively powerless nation. One can easily compare any of the European countries today with the might and resources of a Russia or America to feel the relative insignificance of Israel in relation to these two enormous superpowers of her own day. Not only was Israel small, she was also vulnerable. Israel continually found herself buffeted; she was under almost constant threat of attack and war.

Up to this point in the period Isaiah speaks of, Assyria has been the main threat to Israel's peace and stability. Fortunately that threat is behind them now. However, it appears there is much worse to come. The Babylonian empire is poised to attack. And that is no small threat to contemplate. Babylon is a gigantic, powerful and aggressive enemy.

At this stage in Isaiah's prophecy, Jerusalem has certainly been saved from Assyria. But the relief is short-lived. According to Isaiah, the Babylonians are literally on the war-path. Not only are they now going to sack the city of Jerusalem, the people, the inhabitants of Jerusalem, have the prospect of being carried off into exile as captives of the Babylonians. Indeed the dreadful possibility has already begun to happen. As far as the Jews were concerned then, it must have seemed as disastrous and horrific as the terrifying Holocaust was for the Jews during the Second World War. Exile, coupled with inevitable devastation, was a prospect of terrible calamity, yet here it was—unfolding before their very eyes. It is difficult to grasp, all these years later, how desperately undermining and deeply frightening such a prospect must have been to their morale and stability, and to their very existence itself.

Here, then, is a people facing an almost crushing pressure. Is God in control? In the circumstances, it is far from being an abstract intellectual theological question. It matters acutely because the Babylonians are just round the corner. Is God King of his people or not? It is a deeply felt issue, arising out of a situation whose effects themselves were quickly becoming painfully and deeply felt by everyone in the nation.

In chapters 40 to 48, through the prophet Isaiah, the Lord declares words which came as a real strength to the people. It is no surprise that the political commentators of the time were profoundly pessimistic. It must have looked to them like the end of their nation. Yet the Lord promises a complete turnaround of historical events. The outrageously powerful aggressor of Babylon will be overthrown by Cyrus, the head of the Persian empire. If that was not remarkable enough, still further help is promised. Amazingly, Cyrus will return the Hebrew exiles to their homeland. That must have sounded not only unlikely, but virtually an impossibility to the Jews at this time in their history. In front of their very eyes the powerful Babylonians were already carrying their people away. How could God turn the heart of a pagan and despotic ruler, Cyrus, and enable him to set God's people free? You would be talking about some real power in the land if that were ever to happen!

The fact is, those events *did* take place. The Babylonians were overturned. Cyrus returned the captives. So God *is* in control. He does reign—despite the Israelites' present picture of turmoil and uncertainty. Yet Isaiah is the mouthpiece to an even greater hope: God himself will come personally, right on to the stage of human history.

The coming reign

No time-scale is given for this event. But the certainty is there. He is coming. The King is going to come to his people. This is the goal of history according to Isaiah.

The God who is in control—in control of the lives of the people of Jerusalem—will one day reveal himself fully to all men everywhere, not just to Israel, as the God who reigns. He is the true King of his divine kingdom.

We have the benefit of living well over two and a half thousand years after the prophet Isaiah. God has already been made known to us in the fullest sense in Jesus Christ. History prepared us for it. But, even for us, there is still more to come. The promise of what we now understand as Jesus' *second* coming, when he will finally be revealed in full colours as God, is confidently proclaimed by Isaiah: 'The glory of the Lord shall be revealed, and all flesh shall see it together, for the mouth of the Lord has spoken' (Is 40:5).

The clear implication of Isaiah's prophecy, which was given in response to a specific historical situation, is that God will be seen to reign as the God of the *whole* world— in other words, beyond the borders of Israel. That is the Lord's pledge in these words of Isaiah. He will make himself known universally. We know that Jesus clearly took hold of that promise and related it to his own return to this world. Therefore, even though God's reign has not yet reached its final consummation, the promise will be fulfilled. But, despite that being a prediction about the future, the certainty of such a promise vitally affects our perspectives and objectives today.

The story so far

God is speaking through Isaiah to a concrete and particularly painful calamitous situation in Israel's fortunes. Yet with his overall view and control of history, the Lord declares Israel's apparent calamity not only to be nearing its end, he affirms, furthermore, that this *same* God is on his way. He is coming to their world and our world. God is not silent, neither is he passive. History will one day come to an end and God will be there. He, the God who reigns, will be in control. It will be the beginning of something altogether new when the kingdom truly comes in all its power and glory.

But all this could simply be dismissed as so much rhetoric, and that is precisely what Isaiah was accused of.

'What kind of God are you talking about?'

That is the question the Israelites were asking. We get the feel of that kind of comment from the sometimes polemical nature of the prophet's language in Isaiah 40. Here is Isaiah standing up making these grand affirmations, but what kind of response might he have received?

'Look, Isaiah, we're in the middle of a war. What is God *really* like? You claim he says all these things. But what's he really like? Has he got any *real* power? Can you honestly say he is genuinely in control?'

Some people must have felt, under the circumstances, that it was a perfectly reasonable question. In response, there are several issues which Isaiah highlights.

Who is God?

'To whom then will you liken God, or what likeness compare with him?' (Is 40:18).

Isaiah seeks to underline a primary truth about God. It is a truth about God's power and compassion: 'Behold the Lord God comes with might, and his arm rules for him . . . He will feed his flock like a shepherd, he will gather the lambs in his arms, he will carry them in his bosom, and gently lead those that are with young' (Is 40:10-11).

By any estimation this is an incredible statement. Two points are being made. They are particularly remarkable truths when you put them together. On the one hand you have the confident assertion that God rules. His power over this world is total. On the other hand you have an extraordinary and hitherto unheard of declaration of God's compassion and care for his people. That compassion is like the shepherd's gentle care for the lambs of his flock.

Such a pastoral picture would be an everyday image for a people living in an agrarian culture. Yet it is none the less remarkable, for Isaiah is saying, 'You may not have realized it, but God is like *that*.'

In our experience of national and international politics and government, we do not normally connect absolute power with compassionate care. We do quite the opposite in fact. Yet this is the extraordinary truth: God *is* like that. He is powerful and yet he does care. The picture of the supreme ruler and the gentle shepherd are brought together.

In some ways we share the Israelites' problem. So often we attempt to scale God down. We have a much smaller impression of the truth about him than the facts demand.

At this point in chapter 40, from verse 19 onwards, Isaiah speaks about idols. The Israelites were well aware of religious cultures around them whose images of wood and metal were supposed to represent a kind of a deity. As Elijah pointed out in a different context, these so-called tribal deities were rather on the small side to be of any use.

Isaiah is saying that the moment you scale God down and fail to acknowledge the full reality of these truths about him, your God becomes almost as useless to you as a lifeless, dumb idol.

By implication, then, Isaiah is asking the question, 'What is your *vision* of God?' The God who reigns is a God who is *complete* in his power and strength. He is a God who is able and indeed longs to respond to the needs of Israel and our needs today with compassion and love. The danger was, and is, of having a *reduced* vision so that our God is a scaled-down version and a little on the small side. But this kind of God is really no more powerful or compassionate than a dumb idol. The question is one you must consider: What is your real vision of God?

Isaiah moves on to make a far-reaching declaration.

The God who is incomparable

Isaiah, in trying to correct the defective view of God which limits him to the status of an idol, interrogates Israel: 'Have you not known? Have you not heard? Has it not been told you from the beginning? Have you not understood from the foundations of the earth?' (Is 40:21). There follows a picture of a powerful transcendent Creator-God who rules the world he has made and to whom rival earthly powers and rulers are merely inconsequential. After that picture of contrasts, Isaiah asks another question: 'To whom then will you compare me, that I should be like him? says the Holy One' (Is 40:25).

On his own admission, God is incomparable; but in what specific senses is he beyond comparison?

Two particular senses are involved. This God is the Creator; this God is the Lord of history. Isaiah says the reason you can be sure God is in control is because of these two related facts. First, he is the originator of all that there is. He is the Creator. And second, he has, by virtue of that fact, the right to the overall say in the outworking and outcome of history.

Human beings do exercise their God-given freedom, but ultimately the final decisions rest with God. That is why we describe him as the Lord of history. It is the same strength of power as Creator which enables the Lord to be the one who finally calls the tune as far as human history is concerned. All history *is* subject to God, both its direction and outcome. This is what Isaiah affirms: 'It is he who sits above the circle of the earth, and its inhabitants are like grasshoppers; who stretches out the heavens like a curtain, and spreads them like a tent to dwell in; who brings princes to naught, and makes the rulers of the earth as nothing' (Is 40:22-23).

God knows when to put his foot down. And when he does, in Isaiah's phrase, he 'brings princes to naught, and makes the rulers of the earth as nothing'. The most powerful, even the most malevolent in their use of power in this world, are nothing before the overall and overruling power of God. However destructive and painful, the system of evil rampant in the world today will never gain the upper hand. The rule of terror *will* come to a decisive end. It would not be so if there were not a God who reigns.

What is the implication? If God is sovereign, then that means he is the ultimate authority, the highest court of appeal. He is sovereign over all real-life political situations and negotiations upon which the ultimate peace of the world depends. Equally, his sovereignty extends to all the personal situations of turmoil and threat we face in our own lives.

The knowledge of the God who is incomparable in creation and providence, if nothing else, should drive us to our knees daily—not only out of sheer wonder, but also because it is nothing less than folly not to trust your very life to such a God as this. Isaiah clearly believed so. This is why he continues his message with an imperative.

Open your eyes and expand your vision of God

'Lift up your eyes on high and see: who created these? He who brings out their host by number, calling them all by name; by the greatness of his might, and because he is strong in power not one is missing' (Is 40:26).

It is possible to have very little consciousness of God as we go through the day. Yet it is equally possible to learn to see the activity of God as being constantly displayed in the everyday events of our lives. How the Israelites needed reminding that God reigns even in situations of pressure and turmoil!

God does prompt us. He is present in the meetings we have with people, in the unforeseen events and in moments of joy as well as moments of sadness and pain.

It is like the difference between seeing in black and white and seeing in colour. If you have normal eyesight, you don't see things in monochrome, but it is still possible to be totally unaware of the richness of colour around you—until, that is, you consciously open your eyes to the wonderful variety of the colour there is present all around.

So in this spiritual sense Isaiah encourages a people under pressure to open their eyes, in a serious thoughtful and devoted manner, to the presence and activity of God. The same truth still applies. We too should expand our vision of God's power and of his presence in our lives, to see reality—God's reality—in full colour.

It is obvious that Isaiah had a personal and pastoral concern for God's people. From the pictures he uses, the questions he asks and the vision of God he encourages, he appears not to be interested in truth which was not applied to people's lives. This major consequence of all he has been saying brings us full circle. Isaiah brings his hearers, both ancient Israelites and his hearers today, to the point of challenge and decision—to a sense of personal application of the great truths about God he has been expounding.

Let God reign!

In their distress and pessimism about the outcome of international affairs, the Israelites were tempted to abandon all hope and become totally despondent. They felt that God had given them up, that he no longer watched over them. But Isaiah rebukes them: 'Why do you say, O Jacob, and speak, O Israel, "My way is hid from the Lord, and my right is disregarded by my God"?' (Is 40:27).

When things get rough for us our attitude can become as defeatist as the Israelites'. We feel deeply sometimes that God cannot really see or understand our situation and we echo the sentiment, 'My way is hid from the Lord.' Either that, or God does not really care about what I am going through, so we exclaim, 'My right is disregarded by my God.'

But what was Isaiah's response to these attitudes? Again he focuses on God himself:

> Have you not known? Have you not heard? The Lord is the everlasting God, the Creator of the ends of the earth. He does not faint or grow weary, his understanding is unsearchable. He gives power to the faint, and to him who has no might he increases strength. Even youths shall faint and be weary, and young men shall fall exhausted; but they who wait for the Lord shall renew their strength, they shall mount up with wings like eagles, they shall run and not be weary, they shall walk and not faint.
>
> (Is 40:28-31)

His message is for those who are weak, those who are tempted to give up when the going gets tough—they are the ones who are in the firing-line here. It includes all of us, from the Israelites who were threatened by the Babylonians, to us in our situations today. We are being offered by the God who is in control, the God who does not grow weary or faint, a power, a real power to overcome. It is a power to transcend the hurdles and obstacles which are an all too regular part of our everyday lives. We are not offered an easy ride, but we will be given strength to overcome in every situation. Our God is the God who reigns, and therefore he is able to strengthen those who want to find his way out of painful or difficult situations.

God doesn't necessarily take the obstacles away. He does give strength to cope in the *midst* of the obstacles. Those who wait for the Lord—that is to say, those who steadfastly put their trust and hope and resolve in the living God—will find in the midst of all their uphill struggles, a renewed strength. In the end they will transcend their problems, as though mounting up with the wings of an eagle. Since God is active in the arena of tangible everyday affairs, there is even a promise of renewed physical vigour: 'They shall run and not be weary, they shall walk and not faint.' It *is* as basic as getting through the day. This sovereign God, precisely because he *is* the God who reigns, is able to help it happen.

This is Isaiah's magesterial divine vision: the power and compassion of God, the God who is incomparable and who is the Creator, the originator of all things, the Lord, the guiding hand of history. In reality this is who we are speaking of when we sing, pray, think, worship: the God who reigns.

Fundamental to the mind and understanding of Isaiah is the thought that to be able to trust God in practice, there must be growth in our own understanding of what God is like in himself. As theologians put it, we have to learn about his character and attributes.

If we were speaking of a human being in these terms,

we would perhaps speak of personality and ability. It is normal practice when you apply for a new job to be asked both for references and to attend an interview. A prospective employer needs to know about our personality and abilities to see whether we are genuinely fitted for the task he has in mind. Isaiah's message to the Israelites facing impending calamity and destruction is that God is indeed fitted for the task of their deliverance. They can be sure he is fit to respond in such a way, because of clearly demonstrable facts about his nature—his character and attributes.

So as we begin to think about the God who reigns, the God who in reality *is* King of his kingdom, this is our starting-point. His purposes are tied in to his character. His activities depend on his attributes. All that God does relates to all that God *is* in himself—his holiness, purity, power, strength, goodness and love. He is King of his kingdom.

There is a negative side to all this. Isaiah has equally been implying that a God who does not reign, is not in any sense a God who is really worth knowing. That thought leads us on to the next stage in our examination of the kingdom. Above all, God wants us to know him. He wants a guiding part in our affairs. Far from seeking to violate our freedom of choice and our self-determination, the God who reigns wants a people for himself—his very own kingdom people. He wants us to belong to him, and be blessed by him—the King—for ever.

2

The God Who Acts

The existence of a king suggests a kingdom. A kingdom implies a people. Central, then, to God's purposes for the unfolding of history is this kingdom, which is to be rightly understood as a *community* concept. The Lord desires a *people* for himself, a community with a purpose. The God who acts has a purpose for a special people to influence the whole world throughout history and beyond.

We have already thought about the nature and character of the God who reigns. So now we must turn our attention to this God who acts; the God who desires a people for himself. This God, by the act of covenant-making, ties in his creation of a kingdom people with the promise of blessing and restoration to the whole world.

Membership rights

What is the basis upon which entry into the kingdom rests? Is everyone automatically included? Or does our experience of this rebellious world suggest that the King would have some extremely awkward subjects on his hands if that were the case?

Does not reflection upon ourselves remind us sharply that we are all awkward and rebellious creatures?

Underneath it all, we all suffer from a deep-rooted antagonism to the rule and purposes of God. 'All have sinned and fall short of the glory of God' (Rom 3:23), as the apostle Paul points out, so there is no distinction among us. A deep-rooted alienation from God which results in sinful attitudes and behaviour is the spiritual fact which dominates all of our personalities, no matter who we are. Biblical estimations of our human imperfection are disturbingly precise.

The remaking of mankind

It is all the more remarkable, then, that the God who reigns—the pure, holy and sovereign Lord of all the earth—desires a people for himself. He wants a kingdom for a King, yet that kingdom has to be fit for a King's possession. But with our fundamental antagonism to God's rule and control, that makes us an odd choice for subjects. A people for God therefore implies some far-reaching human changes. But why would God go to all the trouble? Why would he expend the effort?

The only possible reason for his endeavours is that behind the creation of a kingdom or a community of people for God, there is a grand design: God plans nothing less than the remaking of mankind.

God has a great purpose for the whole world. That purpose is to reverse the catastrophic effects of the fall, and to re-establish God's rule in the lives of men and women throughout and for all the ages to come. This is the God who acts decisively in human history to restore to the world the reign of God in the lives of men and women everywhere. In a real sense God desires to establish his kingdom in a single grand design, bringing both salvation and a final outcome of total transformation for humanity by the remaking of mankind.

Covenant relationships

A picture of a bride on her wedding day, beautifully dressed for her husband, reminds us of the poignantly sad fact that marriages do not always turn out to be full of happiness and joy. Estrangement does happen. Separation and divorce do take place. It is one of the saddest and most painful of human experiences when there is an estrangement like this. Such a breakdown of relationships can cause deep and bitter pain for many years to come.

It is a special privilege, then, to be involved with those who succeed in mending their relationships, in rebuilding their marriages. There is no doubt it certainly can and does happen. It is marvellous when a marriage is remade, when the couple are reconciled to each other. Reconciliation is a deep and profoundly healing human process, with implications for every aspect and level of our lives.

Such an understanding of human relationships can give us a clearer insight into the biblical thinking behind the covenant itself. For the question of relationship is at the very heart of the necessity of a covenant.

Central to the meaning of the covenant are two ideas: estrangement and reconciliation. They are the two basic elements. In a sentence: the covenant is to do with the mending of a broken relationship.

Covenant perspectives

Some people insist on reading the last page of a novel or a thriller before they arrive at the end of the book. It is because either they cannot stand the suspense or they feel they need to know how it all turns out in the end in order to make sense of what happens in between. Whatever we may feel about literary cheating, it is indeed the case when we come to the Bible that we are positively encouraged to find out about the beginning and the ending of the story—so that what comes in between will be in far clearer perspective for us.

This is why right at the beginning of the Bible, in Genesis 3, we learn of the reality of the fall. It is a question of relationships. It is all to do with estrangement: man's estrangement from the God who has created and loved him. And in Revelation 21, the 'last page' of the Bible, we see that reconciliation has taken place, and the relationship between God and man has been restored:

> I saw a new heaven and a new earth, for the first heaven and the first earth had passed away . . . I saw the Holy City, the new Jerusalem, coming down out of heaven from God, prepared as a bride beautifully dressed for her husband . . . 'Now the dwelling of God is with men, and he will live with them. They will be his people, and God himself will be with them and be their God.'
>
> (Rev 21:1-3 NIV).

These are the essential perspectives of the covenant: the beginning and ending, estrangement and reconciliation. The covenant is God's single-minded agreement to restore the estranged relationship between man and himself. This is the essence of salvation. The estrangement began at the beginning of man's pre-history. The reconciliation will be fulfilled in the completest sense at a point still in the future. Because it is to do with relationships, it involves God with a people, a kingdom for a King.

Before we look at the biblical covenants in action, however, we need to go further into what precisely constitutes a covenant, and how the parties to a biblical covenant relate to one another.

The nature of a covenant

Covenant-making is a common part of our everyday experience. We may only rarely use the term covenant, yet the activity of making agreements under a wide variety of circumstances illustrates clearly that the covenant is a normal part of our day-to-day transactions with others. There is a principle at work behind all this. It is to do with agreement—the agreement which seals a relationship of co-operation. Without that agreement, there is no belonging or working together. Unless you say the words 'I will', there can be no marriage. There has to be an agreement: it seals the relationship of belonging and co-operation.

This is the nature of a covenant. But a covenant implies the existence of people, parties to an agreement. How do the parties to a covenant relate to each other? In everyday life, the kinds of covenant or agreement or contract most of us are involved in are *two*-sided. The ladies get a chance to say 'I will', as well as the gentlemen. If you sign and exchange contracts for a house, two parties have obligations within those covenants. All these examples of covenants are *two*-sided.

By contrast God's covenants are *one*-sided—they are unilateral rather than bilateral. God's covenant is designed to bring us into relationship with himself. It is *his* decision. It depends on *him* to make it possible. *We* have nothing we can contribute. In that sense it is a one-sided covenant, God's unilateral agreement, the King's decree. A contrast may help us to understand this better. If you order some goods from a department store, they agree to provide the goods themselves, and you agree to pay them whatever the agreed charge will be. It is a *two*-sided agreement. But God's covenant is on a different basis. We have *nothing* to contribute in payment. He comes up with the goods. We simply accept what he offers us.

There are important questions about how we live in response to this unilateral covenant agreement and we shall want to come on to them later. But for the moment we should note this important issue for kingdom thinking. God's covenant is one-sided. He alone has instituted it and promised to carry out its obligations. Its effectiveness does not depend on us. It is a unilateral arrangement which brings us the possibility of a relationship with himself. We must willingly enter that relationship, however, because without an agreement there can be no relationship.

Which one did you say?

When we speak of the covenant, we have to be careful. We need to be clear about precisely which covenant we mean. The Bible has many references to covenants, so it is important to get our bearings straight, otherwise all sorts of confusion can arise. It would be rather like saying how much you like Strauss waltzes. What you mean would not be clear. Someone would be bound to ask, 'Which particular Strauss do you mean?', as there are three different *Johann* Strausses, then one Edward and one Joseph all in the same family. Just to confuse matters, there is also Richard Strauss, the famous composer of *Der Rosenkavalier*, who is no relation to the others, and neither did he write waltzes, or not many of them. So, that's six Strausses in all. No wonder music-lovers get confused!

When we come to speak about the covenant, therefore, we equally must ask: Which one do you mean? If we stick only to the Old Testament for the moment, there are four: the Noachic covenant, the Abrahamic covenant, the Mosaic covenant and the Davidic covenant. So which covenant *do* we mean? We will look at each in turn.

The four Old Testament covenants

1. The Noachic covenant reveals the mercy of God

Covenant history begins with Noah. The Noachic covenant is the covenant of mercy. It is made with Noah by God. It is a one-sided agreement. Genesis 9:8-17 records the main details. God promises never again to flood the earth. He pledges himself to replace his wrath and judgement with mercy. This covenant, then, is clearly still in force.

The process has begun. Estrangement is giving way to reconciliation. As the fault is on one side, and the capacity for restoration is similarly one-sided, so this is a covenant of *mercy*. It reminds us that all God's dealings with man rest upon his mercy, which ultimately finds fullest expression in Jesus' death on the cross. The cross more forcibly than anything else speaks to us of the *cost* of mercy. There is no sense in the Bible in which mercy

is seen as a passive act. The covenant of mercy made
with Noah committed God to a profoundly sacrificial,
costly and painful fulfilment to this covenant promise.

The history of the world could have taken a vastly
different and terminal course but for this covenant. In
his mercy God did something about our sin-dominated
situation—even though ultimately it cost him the life of
his Son.

The covenant of mercy is the foundation for the
covenant of grace. This is the next stage in God's dealings with mankind: to restore the relationship; to
change it from estrangement to reconciliation.

2. *The Abrahamic covenant reveals the grace of God*

> God said to [Abram], 'Behold, my covenant is with you,
> and you shall be the father of a multitude of nations. No
> longer shall your name be Abram, but your name shall be
> Abraham; for I have made you the father of a multitude of
> nations . . . And I will establish my covenant between me
> and you and your descendants after you throughout their
> generations for an everlasting covenant, to be God to you
> and your descendants after you.'
>
> (Gen 17:3-5, 7)

In this passage God's self-declaration of what he is going
to do is very clear. Like all covenant legislation (with one
important exception which we shall examine later) the
covenant here is unilateral. God himself is declaring
what *he* will do. It reveals *his* grace, because only *he* can
do it. It assumes an attitude of mercy, because of the
Noachic covenant already legislated. And, above all, it
shows forth the richness of God's love in its promise that
God will bless. 'I will bless you, and make your name
great, so that you will be a blessing' (Gen 12:2).

When compared with their rich Hebrew counterparts,
our own everyday use of the words 'bless' and 'blessing'
are very poor relations indeed. God's promise to bless is
a far-reaching, dynamic and saving concept. Indeed it is
a pity our overworked English use of the terms provides
such a watered-down equivalent for so powerful a

promised divine activity.

What is it that gives the covenant of *grace*, with this promised dynamic sense of blessing, its characteristic power—not just in action, but in scope, breadth and vision?

Those who work in marketing or advertising are rarely happier than when they can present a product as being unrestricted in its usefulness and effectively indestructible. 'Useful for the whole family,' they say confidently. 'Virtually unbreakable. Should last for ever.' So run the slogans. In practice, universal application and everlasting power may not be such *common* characteristics of marketable products; but by contrast, they *are* in reality the two distinctive attributes of the Abrahamic covenant. These two important elements require further exploration.

The covenant made with Abraham is universal. 'You shall be the father of a multitude of nations' (Gen 17:4). For Abraham to hear those words, and for his descendants to read and meditate upon them for many hundreds of years after, must have come as a profoundly mind-expanding thought. What did it mean? If you wanted to paraphrase it into the very simplest terms, you might say God created Judaism, or more properly the Hebrew religion of the Old Testament, in order to create Christianity.

Some Christians have the entirely erroneous impression that Judaism failed, so God dreamt up Christianity instead. This is a subtle distortion of the truth. The facts tell an altogether different story. Some Jewish people are equally out of tune with the Bible when they claim that Judaism is meant to last *as* Judaism for ever, and that by and large Judaism has little to do with anyone who is not born a Jew. That is just as much of a serious distortion, and the truth needs to be clearly restated.

For Christians and Jews of these persuasions, the Old Testament speaks a clearly correcting word. Genesis 17:4 shows in detail the nature of God's promise. Abraham is to be the father of *many* nations. He is the founding father of a long line, stretching beyond Israel to a *multitude* of nations. The scope is breath-taking. What a vision. To India, Russia, Spain, Great Britain, the United States, Ethiopia, Jubuti, Italy and New Zealand, in fact to anywhere where there are true believers in this same God—the God of Abraham, the God and Father of Jesus Christ—this universal promise to Abraham is extended: 'You shall be the father of a multitude of nations.'

The universal nature of this covenant with Abraham was built in from the very beginning. Christians and Jews must both sit up and take note. For we see here something important about the economy of God. God does not go in for false starts or failures. The work of salvation is destined to be effective for ever.

The covenant made with Abraham is everlasting. 'I will establish my covenant between me and you and your descendants after you throughout their generations for an everlasting covenant, to be God to you and to your descendants after you' (Gen 17:7).

The covenant which God made with Abraham still stands today—because God designed it to be everlasting. The people of Old Testament times were often wayward, as we are, yet the religion of Old Testament times did not fail. Only the ceremonial practices of Old Testament legislation have been superseded.

Along with the economy of God we see at work here the *educative process* of God. The Lord wants to create a people for himself. Such a people need to learn the ways of God. In this way God created the religion of the Hebrews in order that Christianity might grow out of a context of God's Old Testament revelation. In the richest sense, Jesus was a Jew. In his life, death, resurrection, ascension and promised coming, he fulfils the promises and prophecies concerning God's saving acts made clearly, educatively and historically in the Old Testament literature.

So it is dangerous ground to say carelessly that the old covenant failed. It did not. God's grace never fails. Only people fail. We will return to this point. But for the moment we should take firmly into our thinking the strong language of grace. God's covenant made with Abraham is universal in its significance and everlasting in its power. This is the nature of grace: it is God's ability to change what we cannot change, and to save our very lives.

It is perfectly true that there is biblical language which speaks of covenant failure. If biblical covenants are unilateral, how can this possibly be? Surely God does not fail? The answer lies in the fact that there is one important covenant which is noticeably two-sided—*bilateral*—in its nature. As such we have much we must learn from it, both in our understanding of God and his requirements of us, and also in our appreciation of the way the unfolding of God's kingdom is progressive and restorative. This is the covenant made at Sinai.

3. The Mosaic covenant reveals the holiness of God

The people of Israel have left their Egyptian captivity. It was a tremendous saving act of God which enabled them to leave Egypt under Moses' leadership. Now in the Sinai desert, God is about to reveal his law, the ten commandments, through Moses to the people. This is why God speaks about obeying his voice: 'If you will obey my voice and keep my covenant, you shall be my own possession among all peoples' (Ex 19:5). A kingdom people must learn to keep the King's commandments. Later in the covenant legislation the Lord makes this principle specific. It is to do with the principle that those who belong to the King must share in the family likeness. There is only one set of rules for the whole household: 'You shall . . . be holy, for I am holy' (Lev 11:45).

This is why, technically, God's laws are called a holiness code. They are household rules. They are rules designed to be obeyed. Obedience to God's ways is a very simple principle. Yet at the same time it is a principle which teaches us further profound truths about God himself.

In one of his films about bringing up children, James Dobson, the American psychologist, points out that the values we have as people are the values we want our

children to have. So it is with love, kindness and sometimes a firm hand, that we have to teach them to obey,
especially in the early formative years. The way we bring
up our children will often reflect what makes us tick.

It is the same with God. His commandments reveal his
own holiness. If we want to be part of his covenant
people, to be held in relationship to God, we have to
learn to obey him as our heavenly Father and accept his
discipline.

Theologians often point out that God's law is an
expression of his holiness. Therefore to keep the law is
to begin to take on the family likeness. A restored relationship requires a changed lifestyle. But the sad fact is
that God's people in Old Testament times did not succeed in keeping that law. Was it the covenant that failed?

The covenant made with Moses is the only bilateral
covenant in the Bible. Yet, as we observed earlier, God
never fails, only people fail God. The prophet Jeremiah,
sometimes known as the 'prophet of tears', expresses the
deep burden of this fact as he looks towards the future
and records the Lord's promise of a new covenant to
come:

> Behold the days are coming, says the Lord, when I will
> make a new covenant with the house of Israel and the house
> of Judah, not like the covenant which I made with their
> fathers when I took them by the hand to bring them out of
> the land of Egypt, my covenant which they broke, though I
> was their husband.
>
> (Jer 31:31-32)

From the reference to Egypt, it is clear that the Mosaic
covenant is being referred to here. The question arises:
Where was the fault; was the covenant inadequate or
were the people of Israel at fault?

Have you ever contemplated going on a diet? Slimming magazines have a fascinatingly effective, if mildly
cruel, way of revealing the truth to those who want to
beat the bulge. Potential slimmers who want to be convinced of their need of a diet are counselled to do some
post bath-time assessment.

The instructions are simple. You climb out of the

bath. You leave aside the temptation to hide your beauty away with a towel. Then, in front of the mirror, you gaze upon your full glory until the moment when you are fully convinced or perhaps convicted of the truth—new light on 'mirror mirror on the wall'!

Slimming advice aside, many people forget this is one of the main functions of the law of God. The law holds up a mirror to the reality of our sinful lives. Only then, when we see our reflection in it, do we see ourselves as we really are.

The giving of the law to Moses was never meant to be an end in itself. Neither were the spiritual life of Old Testament times nor Hebrew religious practices in general meant or designed to be an end in themselves or to go on for ever. They were meant to highlight the sinfulness of man before a holy God, and reflect a clear need for radical surgery upon man's wayward path.

Many centuries later, coming from a sincere and dedicated Jewish background, the apostle Paul expresses this dilemma about the law:

> When I want to do good, evil is right there with me. For in my inner being I delight in God's law; but I see another law at work in the members of my body, waging war against the law of my mind and making me a prisoner of the law of sin at work within my members. What a wretched man I am! Who will rescue me from this body of death?
>
> (Rom 7:21-24 NIV)

As he says earlier: 'I would not have known what sin was except through the law' (Rom 7:7 NIV). The law revealed to Paul, as it reveals to us, that we need the grace of God. As a people at fault, we need nothing less than the mercy of God if we are to remain in relationship with him.

So we see that the Mosaic covenant, through the mirror of the law, did reveal the failure of the people to obey God. At the heart of all this lies a deep inability: an inability to *keep* the law. The law was meant to show them the holiness of God. It was meant to be a mirror to their sin, as it is meant for us today. It was never meant to be a means of salvation itself.

The covenant made with Noah speaks powerfully of God's mercy. The covenant made with Abraham is ever-lasting. The covenant made with Moses is simply incomplete. It was always meant to find its completion in Christ himself. Here, then, we must return to the over-view of the biblical story. God's strategy, whose out-working we are witnessing in human history, is to return man from estrangement and restore him to fellowship with the Lord himself. He is working to re-establish his rule, the kingdom of God.

However, before we move on to the new covenant itself, where the fulfilment Jesus brings is made explicit, there is a further important Old Testament covenant which we must examine for the development of our insight into the nature of the unfolding kingdom.

4. The Davidic covenant reveals the kingdom of God

If David had lived and died in one of the great modern Western democracies, there would be no difficulty in finding statues and memorials to him practically every-where you looked. In London, Washington, Brussels, Paris, or wherever it might be, a statue, a library, an institute or a centre of worship—preserving and extol-ling the great name of David—would be an obvious part of the cultural, political and religious landscape. Such memorials are a measure of esteem. This is a heritage and inheritance which powerfully symbolizes both his-tory and hope: a nation's proud past and a dynamic inspiration for the future.

The age of David was regarded by the Jews who lived after him, and the biblical writers themselves, as nothing short of the Golden Age. Here is the king who put Israel on the map, 'the sweet psalmist of Israel' (2 Sam 23:1) and 'a man after [God's] own heart' (1 Sam 13:14): the king whose zeal for the Lord caused him to reform the religious life of Israel in such a way as to bring deep and lasting spiritual benefit for many centuries. Such is David's importance that any messianic hope that was to arise from Israel and that promised to herald the age of blessing, would now, inevitably, be seen in Davidic terms. From now on one might say the Messiah has been named. He is to be the 'Son of David'.

In the New Testament's fifty-eight references to David, the clearest link is drawn, in precisely this way, between Jesus and David. Paul speaks of Jesus as being 'descended from David according to the flesh' (Rom 1:3). And Jesus himself is recorded by John as saying: 'I am the root and the offspring of David' (Rev 22:16). David, the shepherd boy turned king of Israel, is one whose impact cannot be overestimated. Not only is his life a model for all subsequent views of kingship, but as far as messianic hopes were concerned his times became a tangible model for the kingdom itself.

Pictures of truth

To understand further how these pictures of God's kingdom gradually unfold and develop, we need to enter into the manner in which God himself has caused the inspired writers of the Bible to use everyday language to picture these truths in intelligible form.

All religious language—language about God and his ways—is analogical. God himself, using language as his means of revelation and communication, has chosen to use models drawn from human experience to speak of divine truths, events and expectations. So in a famous passage (Is 53:1), Isaiah speaks of 'the *arm* of the Lord' and in the New Testament Jesus, referring to the kingdom, speaks graphically of the *finger* of God (Lk 11:20) while the apostle Paul can speak of God's right *hand* (Rom 8:34). Yet we know that God in himself, in the ancient phrases of the *Book of Common Prayer*, has neither 'body, parts, nor passions'. Only by *extension* of thought does this human language drawn from our own general life experience speak of God's purpose, action and authority. The language is analogical: it communicates by means of analogies drawn from our human experience. So if I want to speak of God's purposes, I might speak of 'the arm of the Lord'. We all know that when we lift up our arm we give the clear impression of our intention to do something. It is the symbol of intended action. By analogy, then, we are able to speak of God's plans and purposes.

The comparison does not mean that what is being described is limited to the horizons of our human perspectives. The intention is far from that. Rather, through revelation, God is opening a window on to himself. By analogy, what we know and say of human authority, and the sense of control and direction which that suggests to us, can be applied to God himself and enables us to speak powerfully of the complete perfection of his supreme authority. In biblical language, the human picture—whether it be of sovereignty, fatherhood, love or whatever—is but a model which, when applied to our understanding of God, becomes a jumping-off point, enabling us to enter more fully into the perfection of truth which is the essence of God's nature and being.

Biblical writers freely use the device of analogy. They draw pictures of truth. Analogy underlies the whole process of revelation, and enables us to see the purpose of the Davidic covenant in a far clearer light.

A kingdom in focus

In order for the people of God in Old Testament times to have a hope and an expectation of a kingdom of heaven, they had to have an experience of a kingdom on earth.

In order for Israel to look forward to the coming of a supreme king—a Messiah or deliverer—then equally they needed the experience of a great king by whom they could measure greatness, wisdom and devotion to the cause of God.

These are both reasons why God chose the life and times of David to be his model, both of messiahship and the kingdom: his example brings the kingdom into focus. David's reign was the Golden Age. Everybody knew it. And God wanted to say to Israel then, and for hundreds of years to come, 'When God's anointed ushers in the kingdom—*this* is what it will be like.'

However, the correspondence will not be complete. There is a proviso to all biblical analogical language; it is the same principle which is apparent when we see a model in the light of reality. So the kingdom of David bears the same relation of imperfect to perfect, of shadow to substance, when it is seen in the light of the kingdom of God. As the letter to the Hebrews was to point out, looking back on all this many centuries later, the reality is indeed 'far better'. None the less, the model, in this case David's 'Golden Era', along with the promise it embodies, is rightly seen and savoured as a taste of the future. It is something special in its own right; but for the time being . . . not something to be held on to tenaciously when the fulfilment arrives.

2 Samuel 7 is the main passage concerned with this Davidic covenant. Israel had taken on a vastly different existence to her earlier history. No longer was she a loosely drawn together arrangement of desert tribes. Now firmly settled in the land, she had become a united people, a nation with a great king. At Sinai, having been delivered from Egypt, Israel needed to be constituted into a nation, a holy people to receive and obey the law of God. Now in their settled nationhood, led by a king rather than a prophet, further covenant legislation was called for.

Neither the Mosaic nor the Davidic covenants alter the people's basic interaction with God. These two covenants are for new situations, not new relationships. They fill out the terms of God's covenant promises and expectation, and—particularly in the Davidic covenant—point us firmly in the direction of the future. The covenant made with Abraham is still the organizing element in God's dealings with man. But both the Mosaic and Davidic covenants legislate for new situations in the life of God's people, while opening up exciting dimensions of promise and fulfilment for a future hope.

Here, in the covenant promises of God to David, we begin to see a picture emerging of God's promised kingdom. God's purposes are unfolding—and his people need to be informed. God promises a place for his people—a place of peace for his people to dwell in (2 Sam 7:10-11). The Lord promises to establish a kingdom over which a descendant of David's shall rule (2 Sam 7:12). The king will build a house for God's name, and his reign shall be eternal (2 Sam 7:13). The unique covenant relationship of father to son, previously used corporately of the people of God is individualized and applied to the Davidic king. 'I will be his father, and he shall be my son' (2 Sam 7:14).

All this gave to the people of God nothing less than a picture of truth, a model upon which to base their understanding of God's promises and ways. Above all it gave them a clear sense that God is active: he is working his purposes out. It also reinforced the message that, as God's very own covenant people, they indeed had a future and a hope.

3

The God Who Saves

Hard times

If the David years were a Golden Age, the years and centuries which followed his death tell a markedly different story.

The land of Palestine may be only a relatively small country (ten thousand square miles overall, smaller than Belgium, about the size of Yorkshire or New Jersey), yet its geographical position makes it politically highly strategic. Herein lies a partial explanation of the turbulent times which characterized Israel's history from the time of David right up to the coming of Jesus and beyond to the present day.

The battleground of the nations

The position of Palestine as a corridor for overland traffic between Egypt, Syria and Mesopotamia has, historically speaking, made the Megiddo Pass the scene of almost constant battle and bitter strife.

It was here in the thirteenth century B.C. after his triumph over the king of Hazor, that Joshua defeated the king of Megiddo (Josh 12:21). The Israelite hold on his capital was not to last, for in the twelfth century B.C.

the Philistines, advancing inland from the coast, re-possessed Megiddo, and the whole of the Jezreel plain as far as Bet Shean. Sovereignty over the area passed to and fro. Solomon was able to make Megiddo the capital of his fifth administrative area in the tenth century B.C., after his father, David, had again here defeated the Philistines (1 Kings 4:12).

Megiddo's heyday as an Israelite stronghold came to an end in 733 B.C. when it was captured by the Assyrians under Tiglath-pileser III. Yet the whole area of Megiddo remained the scene of continuing strife. This is where King Josiah of Judah fell in battle against Pharoh Necho of Egypt; Napoleon defeated the Turks there in 1799, as did General Allenby in 1917. Again, in 1948, it was here that the Israelis halted the Arab push towards Haifa. The Megiddo plain is a striking visual reminder of the turbulent history of struggle, conflict and bitter strife which has dominated the history of Israel down the centuries, right up to this present day.

A small nation such as Israel had scant resources when compared with the Syrian or Egyptian armies. Politically, it is against all the odds that in the end Israel survived at all. Yet God preserved his people, for they are a people under the covenant, a people with a divine purpose, and their God is a God who saves.

The people of this covenant-saving God do indeed have a future and a hope. However, for the majority of the Israelites, it must have been painful and difficult to believe that during the unsettling years of depression, the years when God's people languished in exile in Babylon: 'How shall we sing the Lord's song in a foreign land?' (Ps 137:4). There were indeed many moments of spiritual disorientation for Israel, when their God-promised future and hope seemed all but shattered by pagan occupation and oppression.

During the uncertain times of Antiochus IV Epiphanes (175-164 B.C.), it was clearly difficult to believe they had an assured future and to look forward to it with hope. This notorious Seleucid ruler scan-dalized the Jews during his occupation of their land, and eventually provoked them into open rebellion: the celebrated revolt led by Judas Maccabaeus in 165 B.C.

Antiochus forbade the sabbath and the practice of circumcision. He forced the Jews to violate their food laws. He even went to the extent of martyring a family of a mother and seven sons who refused to defile themselves by eating pork. Antiochus introduced ritual prostitution into the sacred precincts of the temple in Jerusalem. And in 167 B.C. he deeply horrified Jewish religious sensibilities by the carefully aimed and atrocious insult of the sacrifice of a pig in the Jewish temple on the altar erected to the Greek god Zeus.

Times were truly hard. In 66 B.C. the Roman leader, Pompey, was given the task of clearing the Mediterranean of pirates. In only three months he completed his work and then, as a kind of triumphant postscript, he marched into Palestine, taking Jerusalem itself in 63 B.C. As a sign of Roman pride and domination, and perhaps more significantly as a gesture of defiance to Israel and her God, Pompey strutted into the holy of holies in the temple, where only the high priest was permitted to enter once a year. It was a calculated blow to Jewish confidence and spiritual self-respect. As it turned out it was only the first-fruits.

Had not Isaiah prophesied about the *supremacy* of Israel? Were not all the peoples of the world to come to *Jerusalem* to worship? The promise was clear: 'Nations will come to your light, and kings to the brightness of your dawn' (Is 60:3). Yet the Roman occupation and the legislature of their puppet rulers spoke only of a steep *decline* in the fortunes of Israel, both of their future and their hope. Their holy places were desecrated. Their laws and customs flouted. Their people sometimes sorely ill-treated and forced into slavery by their Roman overlords.

The times, they are a'changin . . .

In a situation such as this, who would not long for the Golden Age to be restored? Who would not look eagerly for a Messiah, a deliverer, a David? One perhaps even *greater* than David? After all, the Holy Scriptures promised: 'Of the increase of his government and peace there will be no end. *He will reign on David's throne* and over his kingdom, establishing and upholding it with justice and righteousness from that time on and for ever' (Is 9:7 NIV).

The expectation developed of one even greater than David . . . In fact, someone to put Israel back on the map, and establish a kingdom at least as secure as that of David's time. A kingdom to last for ever. A kingdom that would never again suffer the insult of foreign domination, never again experience the blasphemy of God's law violated and never again be ground into the dust by pagan oppressors, for they were God's own chosen people. The kingdom would be one where Israel could fulfil her destiny and, in truth, be a light to the nations.

There was a sense that the times were changing. There was a sense abroad that a turning-point in history had been reached. Messiah-talk was an everyday occurrence: 'Who will it be?' 'Who is going to deliver Israel?' It was on everyone's lips. The leader writers talked of nothing else. It was the No 1 political issue.

The popular feeling grew and became increasingly militant and nationalistic. Israel needed a king, but not a Roman puppet like Herod. He would need to be a king who would bump the Romans on their aristocratic foreign noses and send them packing to the place where they belong.

Freedom fighters

This ongoing series of interrelated events and expectations forms the political background against which the New Testament is written; the background of anticipation and concern with which Jesus had to cope and respond in his three-year public ministry in Palestine.

The most politically active Jews of the first century A.D. were the Zealots. They were the real freedom fighters of their time. As far as the Zealots were concerned, if Israel were to have a Messiah, then freedom from the despotic Romans would be uppermost in his manifesto.

Many of the Zealots' other ideas were right and good. God is concerned for justice, the poor and the underprivileged, for peace and human rights. So in relation to this background, the issue became clearly focused. At the time of Jesus the political temperature was such that the Messiah equalled a national hero—one who would boot out the Romans—in short, a saviour for Israel.

Root causes

Many years before these most troubled times in Israel's fortunes, the prophet Jeremiah made it clear that the God who saves has a different set of priorities altogether. The Lord who has called Israel to be his special people, bound them to himself by a solemn covenant, revealed to them his law, his name, character and ways, the Lord's priority is to transform his people. The root cause of man's disarray, so evident in social and political terms, is evidenced in man's broken relationship with God, which it is the promise of the covenant to repair. *That* is God's priority.

The education process

Christians reading the Old Testament sometimes feel a sense of embarrassment or discomfort when they come across the sacrificial system and the complex paraphernalia of tabernacle and temple worship. Isn't this religion with a capital R? Isn't it rather primitive? Isn't it a relief that Jesus and the love principle has taken over from the God of wrath and the pools of blood of Old Testament times? So runs the ministry of *dis*information.

A *superficial* reading of the Old Testament can certainly give this impression. But a failure to enter into the world of Old Testament times results in a kind of blindness to the education process which God used to teach his people about man and his relationship to God.

That some of the biblical facts are unpalatable shouldn't surprise us. There is something deeply wrong at the heart of man. This is why some of the visual aids involved in the teaching process make us uneasy. They speak to us of our marred human condition, which we spend a great deal of our energies seeking to forget. If we don't like the shedding of blood, it should remind us of the horror with which God looks upon sin.

Written in blood

What does the sacrificial system teach us? From the very beginning of the Bible and Abel's offering in Genesis 4:4, right through to the death of Jesus (see Heb 9:11-14), an inter-relationship between the shedding of blood and personal interaction with a holy God is clearly taught. The truth about man and God is written in blood so that its message should be unmistakable.

In Leviticus 17:11 the Old Testament itself provides a key to understanding this principle: 'For the life of a creature is in the blood, and I have given it to you to make atonement for yourselves on the altar; it is the blood that makes atonement for one's life' (NIV).

The *first* teaching point is that blood makes atonement. It pays off the debt of sin. The *second* teaching point is that it does this by the payment of a life. The flowing blood was a powerful symbol and demonstration that life has been terminated and taken in substitution as payment for the guilt-stained life of a sinner.

Such was the effectiveness of the sacrifices God provided that Isaiah can say: 'Though your sins are like scarlet, they shall be as white as snow; though they are red as crimson, they shall be like wool' (Is 1:18 NIV). Scarlet and crimson are the fast colours used for dyeing white wool. The implication is, since they *are* fast colours, only God can wash them out. The sacrifices were effective because God provided them: 'I have given it to you to make atonement for yourselves.'

But those sacrifices were only effective because they relied on a greater sacrifice to come. They were educative in that they taught the people about the seriousness of sin, the holiness of God and the necessity of atonement. They also taught the people to look forward to a final deliverance, to the One who would be 'pierced for our transgressions . . . crushed for our iniquities', one upon whom the Lord would lay 'the iniquity of us all' (Is 53:5-6 NIV). That such a deliverance was necessary is one of the main teaching burdens of the Pentateuch, the first five books of the Bible, and especially Leviticus.

First things first

God has made a covenant with his people. He longs to establish his kingdom, the rule of God in the lives of men. In the Golden Age of David, we have already been given a foretaste of what that might be like. But first things first. Root causes must be dealt with. Covenant promises must be fulfilled. Action is required at the points where repair is needed. Then, and only then, can man be brought into a fit state when the kingdom can really come, since, as Jesus pointed out, the kingdom of God begins within you—at the level of motivation and commitment. It is a question of who rules. If the kingdom is to come, then God must rule. And that means changes.

All change

'The time is coming,' declares the Lord, 'when I will make a new covenant with the house of Israel and with the house of Judah . . . I will put my law in their minds and write it on their hearts. I will be their God, and they will be my people.'
(Jer 31:31,33)

'I will make a new covenant' (Jer 31:31). This is God's promise. Its outcome is spelt out in clear kingdom terminology: 'I will be their God, and they shall be my people' (Jer 31:33). We have to remember that covenant and kingdom go together. The one describes the privilege of relationship; the other, the consequential reality of God's rule or dominion.

The changes God announces through Jeremiah go to the heart of the matter. They show that when God saves, he saves effectively. He is not content with surface matters. It is what is underneath which counts. It was easy for the battered and beleaguered Jews of Jesus' time to forget this fact, and bypass the need for major surgery. The Davidic covenant could not be fulfilled until what was wrong with the observance of the Mosaic covenant had been righted. When God comes in salvation, this is what he will do; through a new covenant, God will effect a major change that will deal with root problems.

The inward transformation

God, through Jeremiah, announced his solution: 'I will make a new covenant . . . I will put my law in their minds and write it on their hearts. I will be their God, and they will be my people' (Jer 31:31, 33 NIV).

It *is* good news, but it is not *new* news. The inward transformation promised through the words of Jeremiah is not as though God had had a brainwave, decided to do a totally new thing and shut up shop and dispose of the old covenant because it had never worked anyway. The new covenant is not *new* news. It was, in fact, first announced by Moses, and it bears powerful witness to the fact that God never does things by halves.

The *Shema*, the great commandment, is engraved upon the soul and identity of everyone born a Jew. 'Hear, O Israel: The Lord our God, the Lord is one. Love the Lord your God with all your heart and with all your soul and with all your strength' (Deut 6:4-5 NIV). It would be a strange God indeed who could bring a people into such a privileged relationship with himself, command such a whole-hearted and radical response of love and yet finally fail to provide the ability, strength and power whereby that could be fulfilled. It would be as useless as expecting a car to run without petrol. You might succeed in pushing it down the hill. But you would not stand much chance of getting it very far down the motorway. When God provides the road map, he in no way neglects the provision of power.

So, later in Deuteronomy, having announced the responsibility of love to God, Moses then makes a remarkable prophecy concerning the future. That it is a future hope is clear from the context (Deut 30:1-5), with its talk of the Jews being scattered and dispersed throughout the world. But the promise is definite and explicit: 'The Lord your God will circumcise your hearts and the hearts of your descendants, so that you may love him with all your heart and with all your soul, and live' (Deut 30:6 NIV).

Inside out

We desperately need to be changed from the inside. One of the shortcomings of the reductionist views of the malaise of man and society today is that *external* issues are so often uppermost in this kind of thinking. They say it is all to do with the economic system or unemployment or political strife, or this and that. All are important issues in their own right. Yet the Bible insists the diagnosis lies at a far deeper level. The outside is only a reflection of what is going on within. Our untidy and rebellious inner lives need to be changed radically and lastingly. Such is the promise of the good news *first* announced by Moses. We will be changed—but from the inside out.

Covenant signs

In order to understand this curious expression to do with the circumcision of the heart, we need to examine the purposes of covenant signs.

When a couple are married, they join hands and they give and receive a ring or rings. It is a sign of their agreement, their covenant of marriage. In fact 'shaking on it' is an ancient way of both signing and sealing an agreement in a wide range of activities involving two parties. So when God makes an agreement, when he makes a covenant, he provides a sign which brings to mind the fact of the covenant—that it stands and is in force.

The earliest covenant sign is the rainbow: 'This is the sign of the covenant I am making . . . I have set my rainbow in the clouds . . . Never again will the waters become a flood to destroy all life . . . I will see it and remember the everlasting covenant between God and all living creatures' (Gen 9:12-16 NIV). It is a visual contract. God has made a covenant of mercy, and he is saying to Noah: 'See, there's a rainbow. And every time I see it, and you see it, we'll remember there is an agreement in force between us, a covenant I have committed myself to. There is the sign for you.'

Covenant signs are special. They speak of God's promises—promises which will not be broken. That is why, in Revelation 4:3, where there is the vision of the throne in heaven and a vivid picture of the future, a rainbow resembling an emerald encircles the throne. The covenant of mercy stands for ever. There is mercy in heaven. The rainbow guarantees it.

Theologically there is a link between the sign and what is promised. Chocolate boxes in sweet-shop windows are visually just the dummy box, with nothing inside. In spiritual terms, an outward sign without an inner reality is a fraud. So covenant signs are signs of grace. God provides inwardly what the sign signifies outwardly.

When Moses, therefore, speaks about the inward circumcision, he is speaking of God providing that grace within. It is a new ability, a new power to keep God's commandments; it is a power to be different inside, to be transformed so that we may love him with all our heart and with all our soul, and live (Deut 30:6).

Fulfilment

Circumcision is a sign of the everlasting covenant made with Abraham (Gen 17:11). So under the new covenant which Jeremiah announces, the inward reality of that sign is fulfilled. What is new about the new covenant is that it fulfils what has gone before, it does not abolish it. Jesus was insistent on this point: 'Do not think that I have come to abolish the Law or the Prophets; I have not come to abolish them but to fulfil them' (Mt 5:17 NIV).

How does that fulfilment come about? Paul gives the answer:

> In him you were also circumcised, in the putting off of the sinful nature, not with a circumcision done by the hands of men but with the circumcision done by Christ, having been buried with him in baptism and raised with him through your faith in the power of God, who raised him from the dead.
>
> (Col 2:11-12 NIV)

Baptism is the new covenant sign which replaces circumcision, since, as Paul says, the inward sinful nature has been circumcised by Christ. It has been dealt with by his death and resurrection—the effective payment for sin—which we identify ourselves with through our baptism. This is where the kingdom begins. It starts within you, at the heartbeat, where the real you is crying out to be changed. A new covenant has been instituted; God has fulfilled his promise to put his law in our minds and write it on our hearts. The outward and visible sign has become an inward and spiritual grace.

Announcing the kingdom

When God moved decisively into history to begin the dramatic series of events culminating in the death and resurrection of Jesus, the full reality of the kingdom promise and hope was announced in an extraordinary and prophetic way by Mary, the mother of Jesus.

We have come to call her words the Magnificat (Lk

1:46-55). This song of Mary is a remarkable statement about the future, including Jesus' own part in it, and it provides one of the most cogent statements about Jesus and the kingdom in the whole of the New Testament.

Star-gazers

We would all like to know what the future holds. The future is obviously a question which fascinates all of us. Everyone likes to have a go at being a futurologist. Futurology, like star-gazing, has become a Western passion of mind. Journalists, politicians and religious leaders all excel at the sport. Sometimes they encourage us. More often, they dismay us. But why do they do it? And why do we take notice?

All of us would like to know the direction our lives are going to take in the future. It is only natural. We also want to know the conditions and forces governing our lives. Are there any certainties? Is there any hope?

Mary's words provide a powerful response to such questions and concerns. Their power is derived from their subject: Jesus and the kingdom of God; they tell of the coming rule of God himself, and what God will do when his power is fully implemented in the person of Jesus.

What's in a name?

Names have special significance in the Bible. In the biblical world they are not just labels. We see that in the name of the child to be born. The name announced by the angel (Lk 1:30), 'Jesus', means 'God to the rescue'. This Jesus, according to the angel, is going to be an even greater king than David—hitherto the greatest king in the whole of Jewish history—Jesus is to be the one in whom all the kingdom hopes are vested. This was quite a claim to Jewish ears. So too was the claim about his kingdom—it will last for ever: '. . . of his kingdom there will be no end' (Lk 1:33). What a message to receive! No wonder it threw Mary into some confusion. Apart from anything else, how could she have a child? Yes, she was engaged. But she and Joseph weren't living together. It was impossible.

In Mary's story, we see God reaching out to rescue his people. *He* is to be the father of the child. The kingdom and the king are coming: 'the child to be born will be called holy, the Son of God' (Lk 1:35).

A day in the country

It is worth savouring the scene. Like any other young girl with exciting news, Mary cannot wait to tell her best friend. So off she goes, down to Judah to see Elizabeth who is pregnant with baby John the Baptist. John has been sent by God to prepare the people for Jesus. The coincidence is not accidental: God is breaking his long silence. He is coming to rescue his people. Salvation is on the way.

What happens when Mary arrives? Well, there is quite a party. It seems that everybody is rejoicing. It is a real celebration. It is almost as though the balloons are going to go up. Mary is thrilled with Elizabeth's news. Elizabeth is thrilled with Mary's news. In fact Mary is so over the moon that she breaks into this song of praise: 'My soul magnifies the Lord, and my spirit rejoices in God my Saviour' (Lk 1:46-47). They are wonderful words. There is so much we can learn from them. They speak of an enlarged vision of God.

In a spiritual sense, we need that enlarged vision. Our souls should *magnify* the Lord. We have to help ourselves to see him as he really is. And for that we need to magnify our vision of him. Such a concern has been the passion of the prophets since the days of Isaiah. It is the Scriptures which enlarge our vision of God as they unfold before our eyes the developing drama of our redemption—the unfolding kingdom. The covenant and the kingdom speak of a mighty God, immeasurable in his holiness, strength and love. The larger our picture of God, the larger our understanding of his grace and power and purposes will be.

The touchstone of worship

'My soul magnifies the Lord.' That phrase is the touchstone of true worship. The next phrase is the clue to Mary's joy, 'My spirit rejoices in God my Saviour.' It is quite simple, but at the same time it is extremely profound. She knows God as her personal Saviour: 'My spirit rejoices in God *my* Saviour.' It is, in fact, the first statement of personal salvation in the New Testament.

Without that knowledge of personal salvation from God, there cannot be any sense in worship, any strength to live the Christian life or any genuine hope for the future. Jesus went on record as saying that it is impossible to see or have any perception of the kingdom of God unless you are spiritually born again (Jn 3:3).

To help us understand that knowledge, to understand what Mary meant by 'God my Saviour', here is how Mary expands on the character of God in these next three verses.

In verse 48 she speaks about *the grace of God*: 'He has regarded the low estate of his handmaiden.' 1 Peter 5:5 is a commentary on that verse: 'God opposes the proud, but gives grace to the humble.' Mary had just that kind of humility. And so she received grace from God.

The grace of God is sometimes defined as the unmerited favour, love and mercy of God. And it is the basis of our salvation. To receive that grace, our inward attitude towards him must be one of humility. God opposes the proud. He gives grace to the humble.

In verse 49 Mary speaks of *the power of God*: 'He who is mighty has done great things for me.'

We have to ask ourselves whether we really believe in the power of God. Is our God a God who controls all our destinies, a God who can and does overrule human affairs 'according to the express wisdom of his own good purposes', a God who can do great things for us? For this is surely the God of the Scriptures. It is a challenge to us as we look forward to the future, however uncertain that future may be. But what a difference when that uncertainty is undergirded by the strength of the mighty power of God.

Mary then speaks of *the purity of God*: 'And holy is his name' (Lk 1:49). The God who is mighty in his power is also pure in his intentions. How unlike a *human* figure that is. Rarely in our world does supreme power go hand in hand with pure integrity. How often we see power and corruption going together in national and international affairs. Yet the one who by his power actually controls the universe is absolutely pure in his integrity and character. Holy is his name. That is why we can have hope for the future. Behind all human events, however dispiriting they may look sometimes, God is working out his purposes with utter integrity.

How do we know that? We know that purpose is good because of what Mary says in verse 50, where she speaks of *the forgiveness of God*: 'And his *mercy* is on those who fear him from generation to generation.' God shows his mercy by his forgiveness. Forgiveness is paid for by Jesus' death on the cross. Mercy by definition is offered freely. And forgiveness from God is offered freely to anyone who responds to his offer of new life, through Jesus.

Topsy-turvy teaching

What is the purpose of all this? Mary explains again in verse 50: God is creating a people for himself. They will be gathered from throughout history, from Abraham's time to our own and beyond: in Mary's words, 'from generation to generation'. They will be a kingdom people, a people belonging to Christ the King.

God's plan of salvation has a goal. It is in the future. That future is so certain that for Mary it is as good as done. That is why verses 51 to 55 are all in the past tense, what is usually called 'the prophetic perfect'. The Old Testament prophets would sometimes describe a future event as already accomplished. Likewise for Mary: when God says something, the outcome is so certain that the deed is already as good as done.

Mary's song is a prophetic statement about the future

and the kingdom. She sees it all in a moment. The whole story—the whole panorama of what God will do—flashes before her eyes and Mary grasps it in a moment of inspiration as her mind is gripped by the Holy Spirit:

> He has shown strength with his arm, he has scattered the proud in the imagination of their hearts, he has put down the mighty from their thrones, and exalted those of low degree; he has filled the hungry with good things, and the rich he has sent empty away.
>
> (Lk 1:51-53)

It is a picture of the whole world turned upside down: proud plans shattered, tyrants toppled, the wretched rescued, the humble helped, the hungry fed. It is topsy-turvy teaching.

This—the Messiah's manifesto—is truly about Jesus, the baby in Mary's womb, who is to be the saviour of this needy, uncertain, troubled world in which we live. The establishing of the kingdom all turns, in the end, on the death and resurrection of Jesus. That is the *final* turning-point of history, the focal point of salvation. It is the true pivot of the future of the world.

And yet to mention the future does bring a sense of uncertainty to many of us. We are only too well aware of the precariousness of the world in which we live. We can feel, and indeed we fear, the acceleration of the unfolding of history. We fear we are being thrown into a future that is more threatening, more dangerous, more frightening in every sense, than anything hitherto in our human experience.

Yet if we do feel like that, while rightly being realistic about the issues which face us, we should take serious account of these strikingly powerful and prophetic words of Mary concerning Jesus and the kingdom. Her words all hang on the covenant promise: 'He has helped his servant Israel, in remembrance of his mercy, as he spoke to our fathers, to Abraham and to his posterity for ever' (Lk 1:54-55).

That is our security: the covenant promise of God which he made to Abraham and his posterity—his spiritual descendants, of whom we are a part—for ever. It is a promise that God will stand by his people. He is the God who saves. He does not do things by halves. We belong to him for ever. And the future is in his hands. The coming, death and resurrection of Jesus have shown that conclusively.

Like the Jews of Jesus' time, we too are at a waiting-point in history. *We* await the return of Jesus to judge the living and the dead. The kingdom is inaugurated, but it is yet to be consummated. We feel that tension, sometimes acutely, between the *now* and the *not yet*. But, despite appearances, our future is secure in him.

As we wait and as we prepare ourselves for his coming, we must be sure to recover the broad strokes of Mary's panoramic estimation of the salvation of God. These prophetic words show the comprehensiveness of God's concern for the poor and the under-privileged, his abomination of pride, materialism and the misuse of power. If God is concerned about such issues then we should be concerned about them too. We cannot opt out of the major issues facing our society and our world today. The truth is that God is King of his world. And the King is coming. It is the message we have to communicate. This is the God who saves. He gets right to the heart of the problem, deep down into the inner motivation, personality and soul of man. God is establishing his kingdom. And when God comes into power in Jesus Christ, he will scatter the proud, bring down rulers and lift up the humble. He will fill the hungry with good things. And the rich? He will send them empty away.

4
Teaching the Kingdom (1)

Expectation and hope

Eight hundred years before Christ, the prophet Isaiah prophesied clearly and directly the coming of the Messiah and his kingdom:

> For to us a child is born, to us a son is given, and the government will be on his shoulders. And he will be called Wonderful Counsellor, Mighty God, Everlasting Father, Prince of Peace. Of the increase of his government and peace there will be no end. He will reign on David's throne and over his kingdom, establishing it and upholding it with justice and righteousness from that time on and for ever.
>
> (Is 9:6-7 NIV)

Eight centuries later, against a background of prolonged suffering, pain and disappointment in their national and personal history, the Jews, still oppressed, longed passionately for the coming of their great leader —a national hero, a new David—to restore to them the Golden Age. The power of nostalgia, prophecy, and political bitterness and discontent is a potent and potentially explosive mixture in the life of any community; this is especially so in one as clearly aware of its own special identity, nature and calling as the subjugated people of Palestine were in the opening years of the first century A.D.

Against such a background of expectation and hope, the impact of these striking words is in a way hardly surprising: 'The time has come. The kingdom of God is near. Repent and believe the good news!' (Mk 1:15 NIV). In such a way, Jesus of Nazareth announced the beginning of his public ministry. If his declaration did not send a ripple of Messiah fever deep into Jewish hearts, then it is difficult to imagine what could. Waiting sharpens the senses. Waiting, as the Jews had done for a period of a thousand years in anticipation of an upturn in their fortunes, certainly sharpens the expectations; but at the same time there grows a certain anxiety and suspicion at the final outcome. Anyone who claims 'the time has come', immediately finds himself on trial. His claims must be substantiated. And woe betide anyone who should choose to meddle irresponsibly with tender yet explosive Jewish sensibilities. False Messiahs are shown no mercy.

When anger bursts

Jesus' announcement caused many ripples. Luke records that the news about Jesus spread quickly throughout the whole Galilean countryside. As a talking point, it was practically guaranteed. Such a claim went straight to the heart of the collective consciousness of contemporary Jewish concern.

Times had been so hard. However, the reaction in Jesus' home synagogue at Nazareth turned out to be more like a rebellion than a ripple. When Jesus stood on the sabbath day and read from the scroll of Isaiah, Messiah expectation was already rife.

He read the day's synagogue lesson: 'The Spirit of the Lord is on me, because he has anointed me to preach good news to the poor. He has sent me to proclaim freedom for the prisoners and recovery of sight for the blind, to release the oppressed, to proclaim the year of the Lord's favour' (Lk 4:18-19 NIV).

All eyes were fastened upon him. Standing before

God's ancient people ('Theirs is the adoption as sons; theirs the divine glory, the covenants, the receiving of the law, the temple worship and the promises,' Rom 9:4 NIV), Jesus declared to them: 'Today, this scripture is fulfilled in your hearing' (Lk 4:21 NIV)! They were so angry that they tried to throw him over the cliff. He was, after all, claiming to be the Anointed One, Israel's long-awaited Messiah.

Eyes to see

Throughout his public ministry Jesus met with two contrasting reactions: ripples of joy or the outrage of rebellion. He inspired either followers or opponents; there was rarely any middle ground. But how much were his claims understood by either his followers or those who opposed him? How much did those who heard him really understand what Jesus was saying?

Jesus spent the greater part of his teaching ministry on the subject of the kingdom of God. Then, as now, the kingdom was badly misrepresented and misunderstood.

Understanding the truths about the kingdom is a matter of spirituality as well as theology. Only those who have 'ears to hear' will truly hear. The kingdom of God is about the rule of God in the hearts of men. If the heart is resistant then the mind cannot be properly informed.

Jesus said: 'The secret of the kingdom of God has been given to you. But to those on the outside everything is said in parables so that, "they may be ever seeing but never perceiving, and ever hearing but never understanding; otherwise they might turn and be forgiven!"' (Mk 4:11-12 NIV). In itself the statement is puzzling. But it is designed to be. Jesus is pointing not to his method but to his motive. The parables are not made deliberately difficult to understand. They are not. But for those who do not wish to know or commit themselves to their inner message all they will hear are stories pure and simple. However, there is a tougher message beneath the surface.

Communication or transformation?

God chose to initiate the process of revelation, to make himself known, through a culture which operates in a rather different way to that which is familiar and comfortable to Western ways of perception and thinking.

In the West we are used to instant communication. We expect that writings or sayings should be immediately comprehensible. We expect to watch world events as they happen. We heap honours upon our most able communicators. Words and pictures are for information: the facts. We want it quickly and conveniently. If you can video it or speed read it—so much the better!

The Eastern mind works very differently. In Eastern spirituality, for instance, collections of strange sayings known as *koans* illustrate this very different approach to communication. A saying like 'Listen to the sound of one hand clapping' refuses to pass on its meaning in an instant. The failure is to write it off as nonsense. The Buddhist or Hindu idea is that its hearers are meant to struggle with its inner meaning. 'Listen to the *sound* . . .', '*Listen* to the sound. . .' It seems strange to rational Western minds. But gradually, through the struggle, the meaning behind the words becomes clear.

The comparison challenges our assumptions about the use of language and the way we approach the biblical texts. Scripture does not emanate from a high-tech, word-processed Western culture. God did not give his word for the sake of instant communication. He is concerned for *transformation*. He gave the Scriptures, and ultimately Jesus himself, to transform living human beings into the likeness of the character of God. 'All scripture is inspired by God . . . that the man of God may be complete, equipped for every good work' (2 Tim 3:16).

In the light of that purpose, those who wish to know that transformation have to learn to struggle with the meaning of Scripture. Instant knowledge, instant communication, will not transform us; only a deep desire to know and do the truth will do that. This is why

Paul speaks of 'the mystery of God, namely, Christ, in whom are *hidden* all the treasures of wisdom and knowledge' (Col 2:2-3 NIV). Jesus spoke of the kingdom as 'like a treasure *hidden* in a field' (Mt 13:44 NIV). If we are not prepared to struggle to find that treasure and let God transform us in the process, then our eyes will not see and our ears will not hear—even though we may have the impression that, by seeing and hearing, we are participating in the truth.

The kingdom is a secret revealed only to those who are prepared to become its subjects. Of course Scripture is always clear to those who *want* to know the truth. It has its own perspicuity. Jesus underlined this: 'If you hold to my teaching, you are really my disciples. Then you will know the truth, and the truth will set you free' (Jn 8:31-32 NIV). As Jesus made explicit in all his teaching, knowing the truth and the freedom it brings depends on your reaction and response to the King—to Jesus himself.

Stories with a punchline

Parables were his method. Transformation was his motive. The kingdom was his theme. Why did Jesus need stories to teach people about the kingdom? If the King has arrived, should it not be patently obvious to everyone? Should it not be clear that this is the one to whom God has given his royal authority, that God's kingdom has come on earth as it is in heaven? Why did he then use these stories with a punchline?

Once more, it is a case of first things first. The King has come, but incognito. His people are not yet ready for him. There is major surgery to be performed before full health can be restored. Membership of the kingdom depends upon it. Isaiah's magesterial prophecy of a divine royal Messiah, the 'Wonderful Counsellor, Mighty God, Everlasting Father, Prince of Peace', must be linked, in overall context, with one who will be 'pierced for our transgressions' and by whose wounds we are healed, the one upon whom the Lord has 'laid . . .

the iniquity of us all' (Is 53:5-6). There are in fact to be *two* comings, if the mind of Isaiah is to be understood correctly.

Jesus was concerned, in a literal sense, to set the record straight. It explains his concern for clarity in all his teaching methods. Jesus used visual aids, stories and straight teaching to correct wrong assumptions about the Messiah and his kingdom, and to redirect hearts and lives back to God.

Not of this world

Jesus corrected wrong assumptions about the kingdom. He said his kingdom was not of this world. What kind of Messiah can he then be?

Jesus' contemporaries showed a great deal of reluctance to accept that someone who drew the crowds as Jesus did, who preached and healed and exerted such sway over so many, did not in fact have a kingdom belonging to this world. For Jews of a nationalist frame of mind, Jesus the Messiah had tremendous potential for a new Israel, an earthly kingdom, a reign strongly redolent of the great times of David.

Their reluctance is understandable. It was a reluctance to accept that, for Jesus, staking his claim to the kingdom would not mean revolution and uprising and sending the Romans packing. Jesus' way was to be a way of peace. A peace which the world cannot give.

All roads lead to . . . Jerusalem

For centuries Jews had declared the psalmist's words, 'Pray for the peace of Jerusalem! May they prosper who love you!' They had contemplated the bitter lessons of the city's destruction in 586 B.C. They had come, not simply to love the holy city, but to see it as the very centre of God's dealing with them as a covenant people, a people chosen by God and precious. Above and beyond everything else, it was the temple and its ministrations which spelt out the privilege of belonging to a holy God. The temple was a monument to the reality of the covenant and the commandments of Sinai. The city lived for it. And Jews died for it. The temple was the centre of the world. It was the meeting-place between earth and heaven. And for Jews the world over, all roads led not to Rome, but to Jerusalem.

Such nationalism and religious fervour, when taken together, form a powerful sense of expectation as far as a Messiah is concerned. In the light of this kind of expectation, Jesus had to make it clear just what kind of Messiah and mission was before God's ancient people at this spiritual and historical turning-point in their national existence.

Demonstrating for peace

In the present day, the possibility of thermo-nuclear warfare and the suspicion, distrust and aggression between the world's superpowers, have focused widespread concern in the form of increasingly common peace demonstrations. Yet perhaps the most celebrated peace demonstration of all time is Jesus' triumphant entry into Jerusalem. In the clearest terms, Jesus spells out the nature of his Messiahship and the coming kingdom. Clear, that is, for those with eyes to see, who will struggle with the message.

Luke makes it clear that this is a peace demonstration with a difference. There can be no peace on earth without peace with God:

> [The two disciples brought the colt] to Jesus, and throwing their garments on the colt they set Jesus upon it. And as he rode along, they spread their garments on the road. As he was now drawing near, at the descent of the Mount of Olives, the whole multitude of the disciples began to rejoice and praise God with a loud voice for all the mighty works that they had seen, saying, 'Blessed is the King who comes in the name of the Lord! Peace in heaven and glory in the highest!' And some of the Pharisees in the multitude said to him, 'Teacher, rebuke your disciples.' He answered, 'I tell you, if these were silent, the very stones would cry out.'
>
> (Lk 19:35-40)

Louder than words

The connection between the Old and New Testaments is particularly visible in this situation. As Luke records both word and action, the narrative is filled with important Old Testament references and allusions. The fulfilment of God's promises, expectations and patterns of teaching, emanating from the Old Testament, find their fullest expression and goal in Jesus.

A special demonstration of the kind found in the Jerusalem entry is something which was previously unique to the Old Testament prophets. It is found most often when there was resistance or apathy towards the spoken message that the prophet was commanded to bring from God.

In such situations prophets often reinforced what they said by a dramatic action. In a picture no one could fail to understand, the demonstration would act out what the prophets had to say from God; it was a real case of actions speaking louder than words. Demonstrations like this were acted parables. Jesus' own entry into Jerusalem is the only New Testament counterpart of such an acted parable. It is therefore to be viewed with the highest attention as to its intended meaning.

Action man

There are many examples of acted parables from Old Testament times. In 1 Kings 11, Ahijah the prophet of Shiloh tears his brand new cloak into twelve pieces in front of King Jeroboam. The message? It is to show that the kingdom is to be torn out of the hands of Solomon as a direct result of his apostasy. Ten of those tribes are to be given to Jeroboam, to come under his jurisdiction from that point on.

In Jeremiah 27, the Lord instructs the prophet to construct a yoke. A yoke is a wooden neck piece by which a pair of oxen would be held together. The meaning? It was to be a sign of the forthcoming enslavement of the people. It was designed to visually impress upon Zedekiah the king of Judah that Judah would serve the

Babylonian king, Nebucadnezzar. King Zedekiah had been deaf, resistant to the word of the Lord. He was far more interested in the erroneous comfort, distortions and lies of the false prophets. Something dramatic was needed to impress upon him the seriousness of the situation and what the Lord wanted to say and be heeded.

So in Jeremiah 27:12-15 (NIV), Jeremiah, wearing a yoke of wooden crossbars around his neck, goes to Zedekiah and says to him:

> Bow your neck under the yoke of the king of Babylon; serve him and his people, and you will live . . . Do not listen to the words of the prophets who say to you, 'You will not serve the king of Babylon,' for they are prophesying lies to you. 'I have not sent them,' declares the Lord. 'They are prophesying lies in my name.'

It was an acted parable. The classic method by which a prophet might bring a message from God at a time of spiritual resistance and crisis.

The city which kills prophets

The journey from Jericho to Jerusalem is about twenty miles. It was a more arduous journey in the days of Jesus than it is today. Yet this journey, in a heightened sense of the term, was a pilgrimage for Jesus. Jerusalem—the great citadel of God, the holy city, the place of action over many centuries since the Golden Age of David, king of Israel—was his goal. The point, purpose and goal of Jesus' ministry would be fulfilled in Jerusalem . . . the city where they kill the prophets.

In travelling to Jerusalem, Jesus was conscious of the resistance and opposition to him. He had been warned by friendly members of the Pharisee party to escape Jerusalem (Lk 13:31). Herod Antipas was planning for Jesus to receive the same treatment as John the Baptist. Jesus was encouraged to leave Jerusalem, and he did so. But he replied poignantly and prophetically to those who had warned him:

> I must go on my way today and tomorrow and the day following; for it cannot be that a prophet should perish

away from Jerusalem. O Jerusalem, Jerusalem, killing the
prophets and stoning those who are sent to you! How often
would I have gathered your children together as a hen
gathers a brood under her wings, and you would not! Behold, your house is forsaken. And I tell you, you will not see
me until you say, 'Blessed is he who comes in the name of
the Lord!'

(Lk 13:33-35)

In this manner, Jesus left Jerusalem. But he planned
to return in order to meet his death voluntarily. And
just like the Old Testament prophets, Jesus planned a
carefully constructed demonstration of what he had
come to achieve. It was to be an acted parable. He would
give a visual demonstration of what he wanted people to
understand about his Messiahship and his kingdom, and
of how he wanted them to respond . . . for those who
had eyes to see. It was to be a peace demonstration. A
peace demonstration with a difference.

Breaking the rules

The wanted notices were up all over Jerusalem. Jesus
was a wanted man. Herod was plotting to kill him
because Jesus was a political inconvenience. But spiritually, Jesus had been of even more offence to some.
The arrest orders were circulating throughout the city:
'The chief priests and Pharisees had given orders that if
anyone found out where Jesus was, he should report it
so that they might arrest him' (Jn 11:57 NIV). They were
out to get him. As far as the Jewish authorities were
concerned, he was an outlaw. Jesus had not kept the
rules. There was a whole catalogue of offences, not least
of which was his blatant disregard of the sabbath laws.
Many sick people had been brought to Jesus on the
sabbath. They had been in need, in terrible pain and
distress. Jesus had healed them. 'The sabbath was made
for man, not man for the sabbath,' he had said (Mk
2:27). Yet it caused an outrage in the establishment.

Controversy

By such words and actions Jesus had questioned the

spiritual integrity of the Pharisees. But not all the Pharisees in the New Testament get the bad press that is popularly supposed. And it is unfair that the term Pharisaism has become a synonyn for bigotry in everyday speech. The evidence relating to the schools of Hillel, Gamaliel and Simeon enshrined in the Mishnah suggests a sincerity of spirituality which surprises most of their latter-day detractors who wish to label and package something which, on examination, is in fact more complex than a first glance would suggest.

None the less, it is undeniable that the majority of Pharisees who represented this stream of Judaism at the time of Jesus were clearly resistant to Jesus and his claims to Messiahship. Was the reason simply that their religion had degenerated into concern only for outward show, with a corresponding diminution of inner commitment and love for God? If so, the Sadducees seemed just as bad.

Jesus echoed Isaiah's words, when he said to them, 'These people honour me with their lips, but their hearts are far from me' (Mk 7:6 NIV). Inevitably, they were offended. It is, after all, a charge which cuts to the essence of what it means for a man to relate to God.

However, Jesus' offence was compounded by other statements he made. Not only had he healed people on the sabbath and dared to question the sincerity of the religious establishment, but to top it all, Jesus said that he could forgive sins (Mk 2:1-12). Every Jewish schoolboy knew that only God has the authority to forgive sins. The implication was obvious: he was claiming to be God's Son—he claimed to be the Messiah.

Of course there was much disagreement about the nature of the Messiah. Was he to be a divine figure, a political figure or what? The Zealots knew who they wanted. The Pharisees had a shrewd idea who they favoured. One issue was clear to everyone: Jesus had broken the rules, so he must be eliminated.

Curtain up!

Jesus told the Pharisees they would not see him again in

Jerusalem until the people would say, 'Blessed is he who comes in the name of the Lord' (Lk 13:35). Personal rejection and widespread resistance to the kingdom of God were the constant accompanying themes of Jesus' ministry. They were the reality of sin writ large. But at the entry to Jerusalem Jesus insists that a particular message be made absolutely clear. What is it that Jesus wants the whole world to understand? What is the message concerning Jesus' mission which he demonstrated by the acted parable of riding into Jerusalem on the back of a donkey?

Two reactions

The message becomes clear in the disciples' immediate reaction as Jesus approaches Jerusalem astride the donkey's back. The disciples begin to rejoice and praise God for the truly extraordinary demonstrations of power and compassion they have seen enacted through Jesus: 'Blessed is the King who comes in the name of the Lord!' (Lk 19:38). This greeting which Jesus receives from the disciples is so loaded with implications that it receives an instant response from the Pharisees. Their reaction is rather different, and revealingly bitter: 'Teacher, rebuke your disciples' (v.39).

The message has come home. What is it from Jesus' actions, which both the disciples and the Pharisees have seen, which elates the disciples so they cry, 'Blessed is the King who comes in the name of the Lord!', yet which offends the Pharisees so they respond, 'Teacher rebuke your disciples'?

The power of the printed word

In the time of Jesus, they may not have had printing as such, but there cannot be any doubt that the Jews were the people of a book—one book, the Holy Scriptures, comprising the Law, the Prophets and the Writings. Jews were students of unprecedented diligence, because of divine command:

These words which I command you this day shall be upon

your heart; and you shall teach them diligently to your
children, and shall talk of them when you sit in your house,
and when you walk by the way, and when you lie down, and
when you rise. And you shall bind them as a sign upon your
hand, and they shall be as frontlets between your eyes. And
you shall write them on the doorposts of your house and on
your gates.

(Deut 6:6-9)

The lives of God's people were and are to be saturated
with his word. Inward thought and outward experience,
family life and responsibilities, waking and sleeping, the
day's activity, the action of hands, the outlook of sight,
the outward witness to the watching world—all is
directed to be under the authority of Scripture.

Right up to the present day, in the morning service at
home or in the synagogue, the Jewish worshipper symbolizes this concern as he puts on the phylacteries
known as *tephillin*. These two small cube-shaped boxes
containing portions from the Torah (the first five books
of Moses); worn on the arm and forehead, the tephillin
remind him of his duty to God—a duty to subject heart,
mind, soul and strength to the service of Yahweh, the
Lord. In similar fashion, the *Mezuzah* is fixed to the
right-hand doorpost of Jewish homes. The scroll con-
tained in the casing has the words of the Shema,
Deuteronomy 6:4-9 and 11:13-21. Fixed to every doorpost (except the bathroom doorpost) in a Jewish house,
it is a constant reminder of God's presence—and that
the home is a place, as the law requires, where the living
God is to be loved, worshipped and obeyed: 'Hear, O
Israel: The Lord our God is one Lord; and you shall
love the Lord your God with all your heart, and with all
your soul, and with all your might' (Deut 6:4).

The life of the Jews was determined by Scripture.
Their education, behaviour, obligations and sense of
history, were moulded by rigorous ongoing attention to
the word of God. As commanded, they knew it thoroughly and comprehensively. You did not misquote the
Scriptures to a Pharisee and expect to get away with it!

The shape of things to come

Many of the psalms, as do other parts of Scripture, give us glimpses of the future. Messianic psalms speak in hopeful expectation of God's coming one. Other psalms anticipate the great saving deeds of God which will signal history's climax and the full redemption of Israel, the people of God.

'Blessed is he who comes in the name of the Lord' (Ps 118:26 NIV), is one of those famous and unambiguous phrases from the psalms which describes the coming of God himself to bring salvation to his people. Those present on the day Jesus rode into Jerusalem on the back of a donkey would know these words as a Messianic prophecy from Psalm 118. It is a psalm which speaks powerfully and joyfully about the day of the Lord. 'This is the day the Lord has made; let us rejoice and be glad in it' (v.24 NIV).

The day of the Lord . . . The Jews spoke of it in hushed tones. For over eight hundred years the prophets and people had looked forward to *the day* when the Messiah would come to his people: 'The Lord alone will be exalted in that day. The Lord Almighty has a day in store' (Is 2:11-12 NIV).

Chapter and verse

When the disciples cry, 'Blessed is *the King* who comes in the name of the Lord,' it is not so much a misquotation as a modification. The introduction of the words 'the King', which the Pharisees noticed immediately, raises an important issue. It poses the question: What kind of messianic expectation was in the disciples' minds? Or to put it in simpler terms: What kind of king was Jesus?

In no sense are the prophets concerned with pure prediction. Yet it is true to say that Jesus' whole life, his birth, the events surrounding his ministry and teaching, his death and resurrection, and his return to history at the culmination of time, are the subject of both prophetic interest and statement in the Old Testament.

The normal nature of the prophets' ministry was to

tell forth the word of God. As God spoke through them, so they, from their human perspectives, struggled to apply the truth of God's written revelation in the law to the whole gamut of Israel's experience. None the less, it has been estimated that over a quarter of the Scriptures were speaking of future events at the time they were written. 8,000 verses of predictive prophecy contain some 1,817 predictions made from 737 separate topics. This analysis covers some 28.5% of the Old Testament and 21.5% of the New Testament.

Such estimates are open to a broad range of interpretation. Furthermore, it is clearly inappropriate to be using Scripture as a crystal ball, by searching its pages for a blueprint of future events. But equally, it does violence to Scripture's own testimony to itself if we neglect the purpose of the significant predictive element within the prophetic literature. Amos, who was a contemporary of Isaiah and Micah, and came from the hill country of Tekoa, was specific on this point: 'Surely the Sovereign Lord does nothing without revealing his plan to his servants the prophets' (Amos 3:7 NIV).

Royal peace initiative

In just this predictive way, the prophet Zechariah speaks in future terms. It is one of the classic prophetic statements concerning the coming of the Messiah:

> See, your king comes to you, righteous and having salvation, gentle and riding on a donkey, on a colt, the foal of a donkey. I will take away the chariots from Ephraim and the war-horses from Jerusalem, and the battle-bow will be broken. He will proclaim peace to the nations.
>
> (Zech 9:9 NIV)

The king who comes proclaiming peace will be riding a donkey. Modern minds hardly register the significance of this, but ancient minds sit up and think immediately. The reason is the donkey itself. Donkeys were not used for beach rides in Palestine. They are given a far higher status in the East than they are in the West. And in ancient times, only in war did kings ride upon horses.

When they came in peace, a donkey was their chosen
mount. A king riding upon a donkey was a king coming
to bring peace.

The king who brings peace

When Jesus came as a king riding upon a donkey, it was
indeed a peace demonstration. Two questions would
have been implicit in the minds of anyone who observed
Jesus as the crowds waved their palms around him and
cried their greetings of joy: If this is a king who brings
peace, then what kind of king is he? What kinds of peace
are in evidence?

Jewish nationalism had its own ideas. The Zealot
party, which according to the contemporary Jewish
historian Josephus was founded in A.D. 6 by Judas the
Galilean in association with Zadduk the Pharisee,
regarded Roman occupation as nothing less than intolerable. They saw themselves as successors to the
Maccabees. Their longing was to send the Romans
packing—and that by force. They were considered
somewhat trigger happy, and were largely responsible
for the war with Rome which raged between A.D. 66-70
and ended in the disaster of the temple's destruction. In
A.D. 132 a final revolt under the leadership of Bar
Kochba resulted in the crushing of Judaism altogether,
and Jerusalem, the city of David, was completely re-
fashioned by Rome as a Gentile city.

At least one of Jesus' disciples had definitely belonged
to the Zealot party. He was Simon the Zealot (Lk 6:15;
Acts 1:13) or Simon the Cananaean, the Aramaic term
(reproduced in the Greek text of Mt 10:4 and Mk 3:18).
Some have even argued for Judas Iscariot's membership. Other disciples' names have also been linked in this
way. On one occasion even Paul was thought to be a
Zealot (Acts 21:38). And the teacher Gamaliel, the son
of Hillel, may have thought that Jesus was linked with
the Zealot movement (Acts 5:36-37). However, Jesus
was not a Zealot, and whatever the disciples' back-
grounds, with the possible exception of Judas, they
eventually severed their links with this major political

force of Jesus' time.

'My kingdom is not of this world,' Jesus said in John 18:36 (NIV). Jesus came as a king, but not as a Zealot-inspired political conqueror. He had not come to be a king who by the weight of military power and force establishes a world-wide political kingdom on earth. That is what the Zealots were desperate for him to do, and he turned out to be a grave disappointment. Instead, he came not to bring political power but to establish spiritual peace.

What kind of peace was this to be? The whole human race is implicated in an outstanding failure of morality. Surely the Zealots were right to abhor the violent abuse of their land and people by their Roman conquerors in the same way that today those who demonstrate for peace are right to vilify the wanton misuse of power by the Western nations, and the consequent threat to world stability and national and personal welfare. Yet the peace which Jesus brings goes many levels deeper; it penetrates to the very root of the matter, where the problem originates in all its staggering and humanly irreversible proportions.

'Your iniquities have separated you from your God,' said Isaiah (Is 59:2 NIV). Because we are moral beings created by a supreme moral God, if we live in ways which violate the way and reason for our creation, we cut ourselves off from the knowledge of the one who is able to help us through the twisting maze of human life. We are held accountable because 'we suppress the truth by [our] wickedness' (Rom 1:18 NIV). Man is in trouble with God. It is only peace with God that can make peace on earth any kind of a possibility.

Jesus is the peace-bringer. By riding into Jerusalem on a donkey, he declared openly both his Messiahship and its precise nature. It was an acted parable. Why was it important? It was important for Jesus both to spell out his Messiahship and to open up the opportunity for response. The issue of response to Jesus—to the King and to his kingdom—is the theme behind all of his teaching. It is the purpose of the gospel to bring us into relationship with God.

The power of esteem

Our view or estimation of a person strongly affects the way we react and respond to them. In a school, an accomplished teacher who is fair in discipline and friendly in manner is more likely to win the esteem of students than a teacher who is bumbling, aggressive and inept. One of the reasons why media people are so concerned about their image is because they recognize this principle to be true. If you think well of a person, you respond positively; if they are rather low in your estimation, your reaction is more guarded.

In the world of music, the great French musician Nadia Boulanger, who died in 1979 at the age of ninety-two, provides a remarkable example of this principle in action. For well over fifty years she dominated the international music scene, as probably the greatest teacher of composition and performance in the recent history of Western music. European and American composers and performers alike flocked to her. Many of the greatest names in music today owe their skilled technique and richness of outlook to Nadia Boulanger's inspiration and careful training.

Why should a humble, somewhat reticent music teacher inspire such a remarkable following with such internationally acclaimed results? Why was she received by heads of states, decorated many times and often filmed? All her pupils are of the same opinion. They held her in the highest esteem. They worked to please her. Above and beyond every other factor, that was the deciding issue. It is a principle of enormous potential. Our estimation of a person can powerfully affect the way we respond to them and what we achieve in consequence.

It is the same with our view of God. How we see Jesus can radically affect the way we live for him, and what we achieve for his sake.

'Once, having been asked by the Pharisees when the

kingdom of God would come, Jesus replied, "The kingdom of God does not come with your careful observation, nor will people say, 'Here it is,' or 'There it is,' because the kingdom of God is within you'" (Lk 17:20-21 NIV). Here Jesus underlines the reaction of inner response to himself as the most important element in the coming of the kingdom of God. This is the reason why Luke links Jesus' entry into Jerusalem with his parable of the pounds. It is to illustrate that a right understanding and estimation of who Jesus is has tremendous implications for the way we actually live for him. It is a question of the power of esteem.

The parable (Lk 19:11-27) immediately precedes Jesus' journey into Jerusalem, and is meant to highlight the issue of response. This response is later acted out in part by the reaction of disciples and Pharisees alike along the road down the Mount of Olives (Lk 19:37-39). But the issue of response goes deeper still, as the parable illustrates.

The reasons Jesus told the parable of the pounds

'As they heard these things, [Jesus] proceeded to tell them a parable, because he was near to Jerusalem, and because they supposed that the kingdom of God was to appear immediately' (Lk 19:11).

Jesus excelled at presenting the telling incident; but he was not just a master story-teller, Jesus was a master point-maker. Every story Jesus told has a specific issue in mind. There is a point to every parable.

It used to be popular to allegorize the parables and find hidden meanings in every verse. But it does not seem that Jesus meant them to be understood that way. When Jesus tells a story there is always a clear and definite point to it. Our task is to search to find the dominant idea he is wanting to put across.

The parable is linked ('As they heard these things' Lk 19:11) to the conversation Jesus has been having with the wealthy chief tax collector named Zacchaeus (see Lk 19:1-10).

Three reasons are advanced for the telling of the parable.

First, Zacchaeus has become a committed follower of Jesus, and the parable is partly in response to what has happened. What does it mean in personal terms to follow Jesus now that discipleship has begun?

The second reason is 'because he was near to Jerusalem'. Jerusalem spelt the climax of Jesus' mission. It also spelt his end. How would his followers react when all seemed desolate at the bleak scene of crucifixion?

The third reason is 'they supposed that the kingdom of God was going to appear immediately'. There is great danger in misconceiving who Jesus is. He was not to be the Zealot hero, nor what they conceived to be a new David. There was no easy way to bring in the kingdom of God. The patriots had misunderstood the identity of Jesus, and that raised important practical considerations for how their commitment to him would work out in their everyday lives.

The parable of the pounds

As they heard these things, he proceeded to tell a parable, because he was near to Jerusalem, and because they supposed that the kingdom of God was to appear immediately. He said therefore, 'A nobleman went into a far country to receive kingly power [i.e. a kingdom] and then return. Calling ten of his servants, he gave them ten pounds, and said to them, "Trade with these till I come." But his citizens hated him and sent an embassy after him, saying "We do not want this man to reign over us." When he returned, having received the kingly power, he commanded these servants, to whom he had given the money, to be called to him, that he might know what they had gained by trading. The first came before him, saying, "Lord, your pound has made ten pounds more." And he said to him, "Well done, good servant! Because you have been faithful in a very little, you shall have authority over ten cities." And the second came, saying, "Lord, your pound has made five pounds." And he said to him, "And you are to be over five cities." Then another came, saying, "Lord, here is your pound, which I kept laid away in a napkin; for I was afraid of you, because you are a severe man; you take up what you did not lay down, and reap what you did not sow." He said to him, "I will condemn you out of your own mouth, you wicked servant! You knew that I was a severe man, taking up what I did not lay down and reaping what I did not sow? Why then did you not put my money into the bank, and at my coming I should have collected it with interest?" And he said to those who stood by, "Take the pound from him, and give it to him who has the ten pounds." (And they said to him, "Lord, he has ten pounds!") "I tell you, that to every one who has will more be given; but from him who has not, even what he has will be taken away. But as for these enemies of mine, who did not want me to reign over them, bring them here and slay them before me.'"

(Lk 19:11-27)

News update

Jesus is going away—like the nobleman in this parable. Eventually, and in spite of opposition, he will be proclaimed King. But while he is away, and before he returns, how should his disciples, his servants in every age, show their commitment and allegiance to him in practical daily living?

The background story

Jesus used a hot news item as a kind of illustration of his point. It was a political story with which all his hearers would be very familiar. In our time it might have been about a prime minister or president; in the event it was to do with someone called Archelaus, one of the three sons of Herod the Great.

After his death, under his will, the three sons of Herod the Great had to travel to Rome to receive their inheritance, their kingdom. Archelaus was set to become king of Judea. In fact Archelaus was almost universally disliked, feared and even hated. According to Josephus, on the first Passover after his succession in Judea, Archelaus massacred three thousand of his subjects. When he travelled to Rome to claim his title, the Judeans, sensing perhaps the direction of his future, sent a delegation to the emperor pleading that

Archelaus should not become king.

When Jesus told this parable he was in Jericho (Lk 19:1). In that city, his hearers were in easy sight of the immensely impressive palace built by Archelaus and the fine aqueduct he had commissioned. Archelaus and his reputation were much in the forefront of people's minds in this area.

The parable uses as its subject-matter a clearly recognizable event from living memory. Jesus puts the action into general terms, then uses the story to make his own definite point.

The parable in action

In preparation for his journey, the nobleman calls his ten servants before him, giving them a pound (a mina) each. In those days a pound was about three months' wages. The nobleman tells his servants to invest their money wisely until his return. But they are not keen on his new status which is about to be ratified: 'We do not want this man to reign over us' (Lk 19:14). It is the same opposition Archelaus found in his visit to Rome. But the nobleman returns, duly crowned; and he calls in the ten servants for an audit.

The king wants a thorough look at the accounts to see how well the servants have used what was given to them. We are only told about three servants; the major contrast is between the last servant and the rest.

The presentation of accounts

The first came. He had traded with the money and made a high return on his master's investment: 'Lord, your pound has made ten pounds more.' This met with approval and promotion: 'Well done, good servant! Because you have been faithful in a very little, you shall have authority over ten cities.'

The second servant presented himself. He too had used the money wisely: 'Lord, your pound has made five pounds.' The master promoted him too. 'And you are to be over five cities.'

The two servants' efforts had seen a 1000% and a

500% increase in value respectively. Neither claims personal credit for the investment value. Each, self-effacingly, ascribes the increase to the initial value of the capital the nobleman had left him. 'Lord, your pound has made . . .' Consequently the reward they receive is not rest, but further opportunities for wider service; authority over ten and five cities respectively.

Use it or lose it

The third servant is different altogether. He simply hands his pound back. It has been safely hidden away in his top drawer in a napkin. There was no attempt to respond to the request to invest the money. The justification is a pathetic whimper of an excuse: 'I was afraid of you, because you are a severe man; you take up what you did not lay down, and reap what you did not sow.'

The nobleman uses the servant's own words as the basis of his condemnation. If the servant genuinely believed those accusations about the king, then he should at least have put the money in the bank to earn some interest on deposit, rather than doing nothing. The money is therefore taken away and given to those who can make use of it: 'I tell you, that to everyone who has will more be given; but from him who has not, even what he has will be taken away.'

The concluding slaughter, the destruction of the king's enemies, is a fierce conclusion. But Archelaus, upon whom the story is based, was a fierce man. The reference may well be to that notorious Passover massacre. Those who set themselves in opposition to the king must take the consequences.

Who's who?

Is Jesus meaning his hearers to identify him with the nobleman in the story? It is an important question, but made easier by remembering that the parable is not an allegory, so every detail does not need to be tied together.

Let's go back to the reason Jesus told the parable. Like the nobleman, Jesus is going away—in this case to

Jerusalem, first to die, eventually to be proclaimed king, and finally return at his second coming. How, then, should Jesus' subjects, those who are committed to him, live in the interim between his going away and his return?

Jesus is not the king in the story. He is not a despot. But like the king in the story, Jesus' subjects also have responsibilities towards him.

Like the king in the story, Jesus will be away long enough for his servants to make full proof of their responsibilities and commitment towards him. Like the king in the story, there is time for those who oppose him to reveal their real enmity towards him.

It boils down to these questions: Are Jesus' followers, the King's subjects, prepared to be faithful servants as they await the King's return? Are they prepared to be productive in the service of the kingdom? Or are they going to take the title of subject but in reality only be concerned with self and individual well-being, not, in the end, interested in being real servants or subjects at all?

The kingdom needs kingdom workers. Passivity in the service of Christ is a contradiction in terms. It is what we do with the gifts Christ has given us which matters most in the final reckoning. Every single person has a part to play. This is the joy of the kingdom privilege. Every Christian is a servant—a servant of Christ. But sad to tell, servants can be irresponsible, lazy and unproductive.

What makes the difference in response to the King is our estimation of his character, identity and purpose— the esteem in which we hold him. We observed that our estimation of a person radically affects the way we respond to them. The third servant's excuse for inactivity was that the king was a hard man, and nothing more than a cruel opportunist. Jesus is no such King as that. None of us can claim that same excuse. This King did not shrink from giving everything to his people. Isaiah's servant picture finds authentic outworking in Jesus' daily living. He was, and is, the King who served. The humility of his entrance into Jerusalem upon a donkey, his compassion towards those whose lives were decimated by pain and suffering, and the sight of his body torn apart by Roman crucifixion show that this is no ordinary King. Jesus is a Messiah who invites allegiance and industry in the service of the kingdom. He is a king who brings peace—peace with God. But to become a subject of his kingdom is no passive role.

The highest good

We have to recognize the accounting which will take place when Jesus returns. As far as our gift is concerned, if we do not use it we will lose it: 'I tell you, that to everyone who has will more be given; but from him who has not, even what he has will be taken away.' In teaching about the kingdom, and correcting distorted, wayward and frenzied ideas about the Messiah, Jesus made it intensely clear, for those with eyes to see and ears to hear, that the kingdom of God depends on the response of individuals to Jesus the King. Transformed lives in productive service are the only authentic basis for ongoing membership of a kingdom where the rule, wisdom and will of God become the *summum bonum*, the highest good.

5
Teaching the Kingdom (2)

How does your garden grow?

The kingdom of God depends on the response of individuals to Jesus the King. Transformed lives are its purpose. The goal of the truth which sets men free is transformation, not primarily communication. The communication process is the means and not the end of the word of God. But how does the kingdom grow?

Gone with the wind

If membership of the kingdom depends upon response and not birthright, a radical departure from the doctrine of racial incorporation and solidarity of Old and inter testamental consciousness is emergent in Jesus' teaching. For disciples from such a background, who later were to be called upon to turn the world upside down, such teaching must initially have come as strange and perhaps unsettling news to their ears.

During all the years of hardship, had not the Jews survived because of their efforts to preserve the *purity* of their race? Had not Moses underlined God's command not to intermarry when the people settled in the promised land (Deut 7:1-4)? Had not Ezra pleaded with

God, in a prayer of heart-rending penitence, when the blatant unfaithfulness of the exiles and their leaders was revealed by that very sin of intermarriage (Ezra 9)? His actions spoke as fearfully of God's impending wrath as did his trembling words. He tore his tunic and his cloak, pulled the hair from his head and beard, and sat down appalled. It was a demonstration of despair. This, after all, was the most dreadful sin for a unique people to commit: 'They . . . have mingled the holy race with the peoples around them' (Ezra 9:2 NIV).

The covenant itself implied uniqueness: a people set apart for God. Did not the covenant sign of circumcision remind the Jews that they were a special people, that God makes his covenant with their entire families? 'For you are a people holy to the Lord your God. The Lord your God has chosen you out of all the peoples on the face of the earth to be his people, his treasured possession' (Deut 7:6 NIV). Who could deny it? Being born a Jew, one was always a Jew. The big questions must be: Does Jesus' teaching mean all this had to go to the wind? Could Jesus rewrite history? Or was this the intention of the Abrahamic covenant all along?

These understandably fixed ideas about the boundaries of belief and discipleship were issues Jesus had to face seriously immediately he began his public ministry. The spreading flame of the kingdom's power and domain depended on the removal of boundaries and barriers to the sharing and extending of the good news to the whole world.

The new Judaism?

Such reluctance to break beyond the barriers of the known has its counterpart in the church today. When Christians feel a sense of discouragement that family, colleagues, neighbours and friends seem almost impervious to the Christian message, it can drive them into stasis. Discouragement, sadly, often leads to a precipitous abandonment of the evangelistic task. It is perfectly true that many today are either resistant or apathetic.

They seem not to care less about God or his kingdom in any way at all.

In our wider society and world, we observe the parallel growth of Islam and secularism in the West and the proliferation of the cults in Europe and America. We live for the first time in recent Western history in a multicultural, multifaith environment. Competing voices and claims babble their wares all around us.

Some therefore reflect on the effectiveness of evangelism—the spreading of the good news of the kingdom —in a world like this. How much use it? Is it really worth the *effort* to get through to an alien society, to agonize over the hard and uninterested hearts of friends, family and those countless, faceless masses all around us? Will the effort even be effective? Some even want to consign the message of Jesus to pure cultural and religious relativism. They tend to see Christianity as a new Judaism, as God's new covenant for one race only. 'Let the others stick to their own gods,' they seem to say. 'Who are we to tell them what to think anyway?'

Jesus had to confront the inherited expectations of his first hearers concerning the spreading of the kingdom message. His words, though aimed at a somewhat different spiritual world-view, are none the less equally relevant to the mission of the kingdom today, at levels of both theological and pastoral concern. The issues resolve themselves into these two questions: How *effective* is the message? and: How *widely* should it be disseminated?

How did Jesus respond to the attitude he had so clearly identified? In what way did he attempt to redirect the expectations of those whose world-view was anything but ready to accept the world-wide nature of the kingdom of God? It is these issues which form the subject matter behind the parable of the sower.

The background to the parable of the sower

What was at the back of Jesus' mind, what was his underlying concern, in choosing to tell this story about a sower? It is important to see his underlying purpose, in order to grasp more clearly his overall teaching plan.

The front-page cover pictures of magazines like *Time*, *The Economist* or *Newsweek* are always a striking and revealing pointer to their major inside story. The newspaper industry as a whole is noted for taking a great deal of trouble in making effective front-cover illustrations of the primary issues they plan to examine in detail on the inside pages.

In a similar way, in dealing with Jesus' parables, we have to realize they are pointers. We have to look for the inside story. In order correctly to interpret the picture he is drawing, we have to look at what lies behind Jesus' stories.

Mark makes this underlying concern, the inside story, particularly clear: 'Now after John was arrested, Jesus came into Galilee, preaching the gospel of God, and saying, "The time is fulfilled, and the kingdom of God is at hand; repent, and believe in the gospel"' (Mk 1:14-15).

This is Jesus' first statement in Mark's gospel: 'The kingdom of God is at hand.' It is what is at the back of Jesus' mind. This is the inside story, Jesus' major concern—the kingdom of God. But the question is: What does it actually mean? The headline 'The kingdom of God is at hand', as we have noted earlier, can mean many different things to different people.

Communication gap

There can be quite a gap between what we *think* we are communicating and what actually comes over. Getting over precisely what we mean can be quite a problem. The existence of a set of words meaning one thing to one group of people and something else to another was a factor of immense concern to Jesus. He knew there was a communication breakdown on a very important issue—the question of the kingdom of God.

In Jesus' time, the kingdom of God certainly meant one thing to one group of people and something else to another. The situation is not that different today, though circumstances and definitions have changed. Many of the Jews of Jesus' time had come to see the kingdom and its Messiah in narrow political terms. It was understandable, taking into account that the Jews had been most appallingly abused ever since the exile in 586 B.C. Invaders and occupying forces had treated God's chosen people in an appalling and degrading way.

Jewish history from the exile onwards can well give us cause to reflect that recent horrific violations of humanity such as Hitler's holocaust are hardly a one-off event in the troubled annals of Jewish experience. Historically, the Jews have been abused, murderously ill-treated and indeed slaughtered by one despotic nation after another. This must be understood if the strong currents of feeling which lie underneath the surface of kingdom understanding at the time of Jesus are to be properly appreciated.

Update on the times

The Romans are in occupation now. There is a puppet king called Herod, an ineffective governor named Pilate and an ongoing cruel exploitation and oppression of Jewish life and livelihood. The story has been the same ever since Pompey marched into Jerusalem some ninety years ago in 63 B.C. Times are hard, and every Jew knows it.

Against that background, if someone arrives and says the kingdom of God has come, it is quite a claim. The Jews are *aching* for a Messiah. They are *longing* for a deliverer to boot out the Romans and put Israel back on the map. Make no mistake, they want that kingdom.

Bridging the gap

Jesus says the kingdom of God is at hand. It *is* good news. But this is good news on a different level to the political expectations of the popular Jewish press. The kingdom of God involves deeper changes than just booting out the Romans. It involves repentance and belief. More than anything, to be effective, for there to be any growth, the good news of the kingdom involves the sowing of seed, and that seed taking root.

There are certain things which must be communicated clearly in order that no one confuses the message and misses its point. Transformation is the end. But the lines of communication have to be open for the kingdom message to be heard. The kingdom of God is the master theme in all Jesus' teaching. The growth of the kingdom must not be impeded by wrong understandings, wrong expectations or wrong assumptions. The boundaries must be flung wide open. This is why Jesus tells the parable.

The story and its purpose

> And in his teaching [Jesus] said to them: 'Listen! A sower went out to sow. And as he sowed, some seed fell along the path, and the birds came and devoured it. Other seed fell on rocky ground, where it had not much soil, and immediately it sprang up, since it had no depth of soil; and when the sun rose it was scorched, and since it had no root it withered away. Other seed fell among thorns and the thorns grew up and choked it, and it yielded no grain. And other seeds fell into good soil and brought forth grain, growing up and increasing and yielding thirtyfold and sixtyfold and a hundredfold.' And he said, 'He who has ears to hear, let him hear.'
>
> (Mark 4:3-9)

No one need be an agricultural expert to realize that something about the sower in the story appears just a little strange. He seems to sow almost indiscriminately. What sower would normally waste 75% of his precious seed on totally useless soil? That is the situation here. It seems a very odd piece of sowing.

We are meant to take the story at its face value. It may help to note a basic fact about Palestinian farming methods. In the Palestine of those days, farming methods were not particularly efficient. In particular, sowing was done before ploughing, not the other way round. So there was not much of a chance to assess what kind of ground was being dealt with before the sowing began. But this still does not account for a farmer apparently wasting three quarters of his seed.

Surprise, surprise

The point is elementary. This is the only field the farmer had. It was not very promising land. It had rocks and thorns and was organized in strips with its paths running alongside. It was all the farmer had to work with. You could wish that he had much better material, but this kind of subsistence farming using broadcast sowing was the only method open to him.

So it is not a case of the sower not knowing his job, and to all intents and purposes is throwing his seed away. It is much more an illustration of the sower's persistence. He is working with very poor land indeed. Other people might not have bothered. But he does. He sticks with it.

And there is the surprise. The sower really does know what he is doing. Who would have believed it? After ongoing, persistent action, the field yields a tremendous harvest. We are meant to sit up and take note. It is *meant* to surprise us. Who would have believed it? A sower, working with an almost barren piece of land, far from giving up like most others would, persists in his task. And to everyone's surprise, the field ends up yielding a hundredfold crop of grain. There is the punchline. And Jesus will have a deal more to say on that particular subject.

Jesus' comment

Jesus spoke in private to the disciples, concerning this and the other parables: 'To you has been given the secret of the kingdom of God, but for those outside everything is in parables; so that they may indeed see but not perceive, and may indeed hear but not understand; lest they should turn again, and be forgiven' (Mk 4:11-12).

In Jesus' time as in the world today, the rule of God, his kingdom, was not obvious to the unaided eye. The average, contemporary, fair-minded non-Christian person has no clue that God is establishing his kingdom.

The secret of the kingdom is only revealed to those who are willing to become its subjects. Then, of course, with the eyes of faith, the kingdom can increasingly be seen and the way is opened for the actions of faith, which implies that the kingdom can become increasingly established.

God wants to create a people to be agents of influence for his kingdom. The fact is, Jesus' earliest disciples had to face—as we have to face today—the reality of resistance to God's rule. There are many who will hear, who will prefer not to have the rule of God present in their lives. That is realism. But it does not mean failure.

For various reasons, from a human point of view, Jesus' disciples might have been predisposed to write off certain people. Maybe they thought that Gentiles were beyond salvation because they did not belong to the covenant people. Or alternatively, when they met with the discouragement of spiritual resistance, they may have concluded that there was no way of breaking through the opposition which their message generated. But they had to be shown that, in the most surprising ways, God can break through all manner of barriers and reach the most resistant of people. Given even the most unpropitious ground with which to work, God the Sower persists in his work. The kingdom is growing and, despite appearances, there will be a harvest. But, looked at purely from the point of view of the ground to be sown, who would have believed such a harvest was possible in the first place?

Jesus' pastoral application

The sower sows the word. And these are the ones along the path, where the word is sown; when they hear, Satan immediately comes and takes away the word which is sown in them. And these in like manner are the ones sown upon rocky ground, who, when they hear the word, immediately receive it with joy; and they have no root in themselves, but endure for a while; then, when tribulation or persecution arises on account of the word, immediately they fall away. And others are the ones sown among thorns; they are those who hear the word, but the cares of the world, and the delight in riches, and the desire for other things, enter in and choke the word, and it proves unfruitful. But those that were sown upon the good soil are the ones who hear the word and accept it and bear fruit, thirtyfold and sixtyfold and a hundredfold.

(Mk 4:14-20)

It is common to refer to Jesus' words here as an *interpretation* of the parable. Although this is partly true, at the same time it is slightly misleading. Jesus is really taking the teaching further for pastoral reasons. He is drawing out pastoral *applications* rather than an interpretation. And it is spoken only to the disciples, not the crowds, so that they will have a deeper insight into the issues involved in actually communicating the good news about Jesus and the kingdom across the boundaries to the wider world in which they live.

The seed and the ground

'The sower sows the word.' From this application it becomes clear that the message to be received is a message to be understood. It has content. It is the word.

Jesus came into Galilee preaching the gospel of God and saying, 'The time is fulfilled, and the kingdom of God is at hand; repent, and believe in the gospel.' This is the content of the message. Of course Jesus' followers must earn the right to speak. The church must be a sign of the kingdom to the world. Disciples must learn to communicate in the widest sense the concerns and affairs of the kingdom: care for the poor, the needy, the underprivileged, the suffering; love for God and each other. Such care and love are a powerful witness to Jesus himself. They communicate both King and kingdom.

The King who beckons

However, unless individual responsibility is taken to communicate the word, to actually *speak* to an otherwise preoccupied and uninterested world, how will the kingdom grow? In the end, the message has to be communicated verbally. Otherwise no one will understand. As in

Jesus' day, so in ours, what happens is only too obvious: people keep quiet. The watching world concludes that kingdom people are either nice or religious. Such silence blurs their vision—they fail to see that the kingdom belongs to the King, the King who beckons.

Silent witness and Christian presence

There is no such thing as a silent witness or the liberal concept of the Christian presence, a kingdom without a King desiring to rule—not as far as the New Testament is concerned. Being kind to people is highly praiseworthy, but it does not turn them into Christians, into kingdom people ruled over by the King.

The sower sows the word. We have to speak it. It is the only means of producing the harvest. Pastorally, there are, of course, times when silence is required, in families and some other situations. But even then, it is as a prelude to speaking appropriately when God opens up the opportunity. (Compare 1 Peter 3:15 with its context in 1 Peter 1:1-2.) There will always be different types of response. Jesus pointed out the importance of not foreclosing the issue by presupposing exactly what that response might be.

Four soils

When we examine 'the ground' we see how Jesus goes to particular lengths to demonstrate the different kinds of responses we are likely to find when we sow the word. It is to underline the fact there are different kinds of human soil.

What does *the path* teach? It is the first pastoral application Jesus made. He was saying, 'Be aware of the spiritual struggle of evangelism.' There is satanic opposition. His disciples, and Christians today, needed to be prepared for the fact that sometimes no response at all will be seen to the kingdom's message. It should be expected, because 'Satan immediately comes and takes away the word which is sown in them'. He knew the reality of satanic opposition firsthand from his own wilderness experience. He did not underestimate the

dynamic power of evil manifest in a personal devil.
There *is* a spiritual struggle.

The rocky ground. There is a certain amount of fall-out
in all evangelistic work. There are those in whom the
message of Christ will only ever be received in a shallow
way. They may look like Christians for a while, saying
and doing the right things. But the proof is whether
they endure. And when they fall away, because the good
times are past and the action has toughened up, it is sad;
but do not be surprised, you were warned. Jesus said,
'He who endures to the end will be saved' (Mt 10:22).
This is why the apostles placed such importance on
proper establishment in the Christian life. It is why Paul
can refer to 'the commission God gave me to present to
you the word of God in its fullness . . . so that we may
present everyone perfect in Christ' (Col 1:25, 28 NIV). It
is indeed playing with fire to settle with being a part-
time or half-hearted subject of the kingdom and so
prove to be rocky ground.

The thorns. We all have to be warned of the stranglehold of materialism. Jesus says the cares of the world,
the delight in riches and the desire for other things can
enter in and choke the word, and it can prove unfruitful. Nothing has changed in this regard from the disciples' time. All of us need to be warned that we can be
spiritually choked to death if we allow the wrong kinds
of material concerns and aspirations to get the better of
us.

The good soil. Here, at last, are the ones who hear the
word, accept it and bear fruit—thirtyfold and sixtyfold
and a hundredfold. And here the point of the parable
becomes clear. The conclusion is this: There are different types of ground, but only one message. And
truthfully, like the sower sowing on unploughed land,
the kind of ground being dealt with cannot be known
until both the word has been sown and that word has
been given time to take root and grow.

Hidden action

The contemporary world is highly results-conscious.

Results are wanted immediately partly because we get anxious and partly because we live in an instant culture. Jesus has a different and timeless outlook. He emphasized that it was important to let growth take place steadily, and hidden from the eye for a while. The action may be hidden, but that does not mean nothing is going on.

> The kingdom of God is as if a man should scatter seed upon the ground, and should sleep and rise night and day, and the seed should sprout and grow, he knows not how. The earth produces of itself, first the blade, then the ear, then the full grain in the ear. But when the grain is ripe, at once he puts in the sickle, because the harvest has come.
>
> (Mk 4:26-29)

Sometimes the process of germination and growth takes quite a time. The results may seem far from instant. But we must not make the mistake of thinking, after the seed has been sown, that nothing is happening. It is just that we cannot see beneath the surface. Something *is* happening. That is why we have to sow widely.

Selective sowing must be out. We cannot know what kind of ground we are dealing with. And we should not give up simply because we do not see results instantly. Every conversion is preceded by God's inner work of preparing that ground. It is his work of prevenient, or preparatory, grace: 'No one can come to me unless the Father who sent me draws him' (Jn 6:44).

People only prove their ultimate spiritual nature and destiny by their response to Christ. The disciples were being told not to be discouraged. There will be many different responses; some will be for him, some against him. Equally they were being shown that what may look like an extremely unpropitious opportunity is eventually going to issue in a harvest. Jesus tells his disciples in his and every generation, 'Do not let yourself become discouraged or depressed by what appears on the surface to be a very unpromising situation. You could be in for quite a surprise.'

Whatever the different kinds of ground there may be,

there is only one field. Until it is all ploughed up, no one knows what kind of ground is being dealt with. There is also only one seed which will make any kind of impact on ground like that. The conclusion is quite straight-forward—the seed must be sown.

Sowing today

We are meant to be challenged by this parable. Many of us write off whole groups of people or individuals because we reckon they are poor ground. Surely the message of the sower is that we cannot tell that until the seed has been both sown and given a chance to take root and grow. Positively, we should exclude no one. Yes, be prepared for opposition. Yes, be prepared for failure. We have been warned; it is in the nature of things. But do not give up. Catch the vision for it. It does not matter if our work is three-quarters wasted. Some will take root.

It is a question of having a vision of the possible. We can be confident because it is God, not us, who converts people. It is the message, not the messenger, that matters. The seed is the word.

A sower went out to sow, and as he did so, he widened the dimensions of the realm of God, so it could be a kingdom extending beyond all human barriers of race, class and creed. Today *our* vision needs to widen, even where humanly speaking we estimate hardly any response. How wrong it is possible to be. We are to be encouraged, like the sower, to stick with it and be persistent. And one day we will all see the great surprise—the day the harvest comes and 'the kingdom of the world' becomes 'the kingdom of our Lord and of his Christ' (Rev 11:15).

6

Teaching the Kingdom (3)

Covenant truth can become obscured in covenant privilege. Many times through history God's people had to be reminded that their special status rested not on merit but on grace. Moses spoke warmly of the privilege of belonging; and for generation upon generation such a standing before God was the treasured inheritance of every son and daughter of Abraham. 'What other nation is so great as to have their gods near them the way the Lord our God is near whenever we pray to him?' (Deut 4:7 NIV).

Yet privilege became mingled with disobedience and distortion. Several centuries later, the Lord instructed the prophet Jeremiah to declare to his people: 'This is the nation that has not obeyed the Lord its God or responded to correction. Truth has perished; it has vanished from their lips' (Jer 7:28 NIV).

The truth distorters

In teaching the kingdom, Jesus came as a restorer of truth. So much of what had been revealed in former times had become overlaid with the thick varnish of hardened hearts and distorted doctrine. In the period between the Testaments, layer upon layer of tradition was added to the teaching of the Torah. Such were the distortions of truth and moral action propounded by influential members of the Pharisee party that Jesus found himself constrained to spell out the issue clearly. The Pharisees were a plant not planted by his heavenly Father. As distorters of truth, they were in fact blind guides. The logic was inescapable: 'If a blind man leads a blind man, both will fall into a pit' (Mt 15:13-14 NIV).

Such an understanding accounts for the constant dialogue, both explicit and implicit, that Jesus continued with the Pharisees throughout his public ministry. Similarities in the sayings of Jesus to the celebrated rabbi Hillel confirm that Jesus was careful to speak at precisely the level of the Pharisees' understanding. It appears Jesus often took a saying of Hillel which would be well known to the Pharisees and turned its meaning subtly, re-establishing the fundamental nature of kingdom truth.

Beyond the strangely distorted ways of tradition, Jesus also had to contend with the calloused nature of the human heart itself. 'The heart is deceitful above all things' (Jer 17:9 NIV). The privilege of belonging had done nothing to change man's inner weakness. There was still the self-deception, still the shallow optimism of self-justifying works, still the sluggishness of response, still the natural inability to perceive the truth of God.

It was not just the Pharisees and Sadducees who needed putting right. The whole human race is implicated in a tragic failure of morality. It is indeed a serious issue when God's own people grow insensitive to their own weakness and consequent unworthiness before a holy God. Covenant truth can become obscured in covenant privilege. There is not much sense in building the kingdom if there is no deep inner conviction of the priority of the changes required within. There will be little sense of urgency if man's alienation from God is not perceived realistically and potently. There will be hardly any passion for the gospel if the lostness of humankind and the impending judgement are not seen as the frightening inevitabilities of our fragile situation. Above all, the loss of such a world-view demotes the staggeringly sacrificial love of the Father in sending his Son to die in the place of fallen humanity to a pallid gesture of benevolent human example-setting. The message of the stupendous love of God, which has been unfolding in Jewish history from the time of Noah, through Abraham, Moses, David and the prophets, is finding its culmination in Jesus. The truth, as a first priority, must be straightened out.

The kingdom grows by sowing. But it is to mind and will, understanding and response, that Jesus aims the content of the seed. For in whatever ways the truth may become distorted, those ways originate in the rebelliousness of the human heart itself.

The long search

The Pharisees of Jesus' time had not exactly forgotten the truth of man's fallen condition. They had simply come to a settled conclusion on the matter. Their exaggerated pride in belonging to the God of Israel had caused them to adopt a hard and narrow outlook, not only to non-Jews, but also to those who did not share their rigorous and meticulous approach to ritual purity of life. Saddest of all, they were guilty of obscuring the passionate concern of God to search out and find those lost in their worldly alienation and guilt. 'God is the God of Israel, after all,' they reasoned. 'How could he be interested in the Gentiles?'

Mission nowhere

This failure to appreciate God's deep and passionate concern to seek out that which is lost has swung to the opposite extreme in our own day. The British television series, *The Long Search*, a major BBC documentary in thirteen parts, which took some four years to make, is a typical illustration. During the period of its first showing, week by week, the television magazine, the *Radio Times*, received from the *Long Search* office what is usually called 'the billing'—the title of the programmes, comprising a few details and a short paragraph of description designed to entice the audience. Only the most careful readers would have noticed certain tell-tale modifications in the wording over that period of three months. But the changes are spiritually significant.

For the first eight films, the announcement began: '*The Long Search* is a thirteen-part world-wide film series on man's religious quest.' The next three went: '*The Long Search*—a thirteen-part world-wide series on man's quest for meaning.' The last two announcements, with a hint of sadness, bewilderment and bemused mystification, read: '*The Long Search*—a thirteen-part world-wide series . . .' It seems as though the long search had ended up precisely nowhere.

Modern man thinks he can search out God in whatever way he chooses and at his own convenience. Four years of sincere, responsible documentary film-making, however, told a different story. Man cannot pierce through the heavens and perceive the truth of God un-aided.

The long search of man is a mission doomed to failure. The distortions of the human heart are his barrier. It comes, then, as an eye-opener to Pharisee and rationalist alike to discover that God himself is the one involved in the long search. God's search for man, who is lost and whom he loves with passion and concern, is an *active* search; in a real sense, it is a mission with a clear determination that what is lost shall be found.

Lost and found

If something is important, you tend to try to make it as easy to understand as possible. When people wrap up their best thoughts in impenetrable jargon, they give the impression that their message cannot be absolutely crucial and vital to grasp. Clearly Jesus was concerned to make his teaching on this aspect of the kingdom as accessible as possible. He chose three pictures from the familiar world of everyday experience to underline one basic truth about God: he is passionately concerned about his lost children and searches for them. It was a truth which had become so distorted with the jargon of Pharisaism that God's love and joy had been relegated to the impenetrable and inaccessible. This was so much the case that strict Pharisees would say, 'There is joy in heaven over one sinner who is *obliterated* before God.'

To correct and restore the nature of this truth about God, Jesus told three related parables about a sheep, a coin and a son—all of which were lost, but then were found. Luke links the three together in one chapter to emphasize how their message belongs together.

The lost sheep

> What man of you, having a hundred sheep, if he has lost one of them, does not leave the ninety-nine in the wilderness, and go after the one which is lost, until he finds it? And when he has found it, he lays it on his shoulders, rejoicing. And when he comes home, he calls together his friends and his neighbours, saying to them, 'Rejoice with me, for I have found my sheep which was lost.' Just so, I tell you, there will be more joy in heaven over one sinner who repents than over ninety-nine righteous persons who need no repentance.

> (Lk 15:3-7)

The pundits of Jesus' time were sure God cared for the Pharisees; they were just as sure he didn't care for anyone else. Popular philosophy today is not sure there is a God at all, but if there is, he, she or it certainly wouldn't be able to care—for that, surely, would be far too *human*.

Is there a God who cares? The lost sheep is certainly a picture all of Jesus' hearers would appreciate. Coming from a farming environment as they did, it was easy to understand.

In the Judean countryside pasture is scarce. To this day there are dangers from high cliffs and the bleak devastation of the desert. When a sheep gets lost the shepherd drops everything. The sheep matters to him. It is not just that his livelihood depends on it. In fact, one sheep more or less is not going to make a great deal of difference; though many of the flocks then belonged not to individuals, but communally to whole villages. It has as much to do with the fact that you come to love your sheep. Granted, sheep are in a way foolish creatures, easily frightened and not that good at looking after themselves. But you do come to care for them. Every shepherd will tell you the same. If a sheep gets lost, off you go, dropping everything, until you come back victorious, the sheep over your shoulders.

Shepherds would often go out in teams of two or three. When, as would often happen, two would arrive back at the village, leaving the one with his flock on the mountainside because a sheep was lost, the whole village would go out to greet him as a community, to share in the thanksgiving when he returned with the lost sheep that had been found.

Luke mentions the reason why Jesus told this parable. The tax collectors and sinners had been gathering all around Jesus, and the Pharisees and the scribes had not made any secret of their feelings: 'This man receives sinners and eats with them' (v.2).

It is a mistake, of course, to caricature the Pharisees and suggest they thought it was outrageous that Jesus should have any contact at all with those whom they in any case found distasteful. They did, in their strange way, believe in repentance, that sinners could make representations of penitence and regret for sin. The issue which really upset the Pharisees is that Jesus seemed to make repentance an excuse for a party. How dare he get so enthusiastic about it! Sackcloth and ashes are one thing; supper parties are another. As far as they were concerned God would be brought into disrepute. Religion would degenerate into meetings for praise! From their sober viewpoint there was no need to get so enthusiastic about repentance.

The only reason to become enthusiastic, according to Jesus, is that God *cares*. If an ordinary shepherd cares that much about an ordinary sheep, how much more, then, does God care about human beings—about any single one human being who is lost? Will God not do all in his power to seek and find that which is lost? And when he is found, is he not full of joy? Jesus' reason was clear: 'I tell you, there will be more joy in heaven over one sinner who repents than over ninety-nine righteous persons who need no repentance' (v.7).

Jesus is keen to underline the fact. Such an important issue must not be obscured. Three different stories are used to drive the point home, lest there be any confusion on the subject. So the same comment is made in the second parable (Lk 15:8-10) when the woman finds her lost coin: 'I tell you, there is joy before the angels of God over one sinner who repents' (Lk 15:10).

The forgotten father

A similar emphasis in the third parable Luke records (Lk 15:11-32) adds a further dimension. The joy of discovery is still there. But whereas the sheep was by its nature stupid, and the coin merely lost, in the case of the prodigal son, he was in fact guilty. And the parable is not so much about the son in the story, as the forgotten father—the father who is prepared to unconditionally forgive his son, and go out towards him, at only the slightest hint of a willingness to return.

> And [Jesus] said, 'There was a man who had two sons; and the younger of them said to his father, "Father, give me the share of property that falls to me." And he divided his living between them. Not many days later, the younger brother gathered all he had and took his journey into a far country, and there he squandered his property in loose living. And when he had spent everything, a great famine arose in that country, and he began to be in want. So he went and joined himself to one of the citizens of that country, who sent him into his fields to feed swine. And he would gladly have fed on the pods that the swine ate; and no one gave him anything. But when he came to himself he said, "How many of my father's hired servants have bread enough and to spare, but I perish here with hunger! I will arise and go to my father, and I will say to him, 'Father, I have sinned against heaven and before you; I am no longer worthy to be called your son; treat me as one of your hired servants.'" And he arose and came to his father. But while he was yet at a distance, his father saw him and had com-

passion, and ran and embraced him and kissed him. And the son said to him, "Father I have sinned against heaven and before you; I am no longer worthy to be called your son." But the father said to his servants, "Bring quickly the best robe, and put it on him; and put a ring on his hand, and shoes on his feet; and bring the fatted calf and kill it, and let us eat and make merry, for this my son was dead, and is alive again; he was lost, and is found." And they began to make merry.

'Now his elder son was in the field; and as he came and drew near to the house, he heard music and dancing. And he called one of the servants and asked what this meant. And he said to him, "Your brother has come, and your father has killed the fatted calf, because he has received him safe and sound." But he was angry and refused to go in. His father came out and entreated him, but he answered his father, "Lo, these many years I have served you, and I have never disobeyed your command; yet you never gave me a kid, that I might make merry with my friends. But when this son of yours came, who has devoured your living with harlots, you killed for him the fatted calf!" And he said to him, "Son, you are always with me, and all that is mine is yours. It was fitting to make merry and be glad, for this your brother was dead, and is alive; he was lost, and is found."'

(Lk 15:11-32)

The Father of the kingdom

Jesus' parable is meant to announce the marvel that God is like a loving Father. He is prepared, where there is repentance to forgive the guilty and adopt them into his family. The Pharisees, who might have identified themselves with the elder brother in the story, would have to realize they had no exclusive right to God's interest. God longs to be known to us as our Father. But the prodigal must show a willingness to return, even though he can bring nothing to justify his Father's acceptance. The forgiveness has to come free.

Quote, misquote

In teaching the kingdom today, Christians face a popular fallacy which reflects the casual spirituality of the Pharisees on this matter. The Pharisees were convinced they had an automatic right to God's care and interest. Jesus' teaching on the fatherhood of God was new and revolutionary, but it did not make any difference to the Pharisees' failure to recognize the supreme privilege of belonging.

Today we are just as likely to encounter misconceptions on this level. It is usually put something like: 'Surely God is the Father of all?' or 'Aren't we all children of God anyway?' It is a case of 'quote, misquote'. The care of God and the privilege of belonging are regarded with shallow and casual thoughtlessness, sapping them of their force and impact as gospel truth.

The statement 'God is the Father of all' is a fallacy. It is based on a theological confusion between God the Creator and God the Saviour. Yes, God is the Creator of all. And in that creation sense, he is the originator of all things. He is the Father in the general sense of Creator. He loves all that he has made. But the biblical emphasis is that the world as a whole is in rebellion against God. It no longer knows God in his kingly authority over creation and individual lives. Since the fall of man, no one has any right to call God Father except through the saving intervention of Jesus Christ.

It is God the Saviour, in Jesus Christ, who has put the relationship right. And it is only those who respond to God through him who can properly be called children of God—children of the King, children of the Father of the kingdom. The Bible is clear: God is the Creator of all, but he is the Father only of those who put their trust in Jesus Christ.

The truth about being a child of God

This is far more than a doctrine. It is meant to be experienced as a genuinely exciting reality. That God is our Father and we are his children is a relationship which simply thrilled Christians of New Testament times. They bubbled over with enthusiasm because they knew what a barrier had been removed between the Creator and themselves. John's first letter illustrates the excitement of this relationship: 'Consider the incredible love that the Father has shown us in allowing us to be called "children of God"—and that is not just what we are called, but what we *are*' (1 Jn 3:1 Phillips).

There is no sense here of taking the relationship for granted. In a real way, being children of the Father is regarded as a supreme privilege. It is what we are by grace, not by right of creation. Naturally we are alienated from God the Creator. It is only by salvation, what God has given us, that this supreme privilege can be ours. It comes through the intervening work of Jesus Christ. Now we can be—and be known as—God's children. This kingdom reality resonates throughout the pages of the New Testament. The apostle Paul in particular makes the Christian's privilege of the fatherhood of God explicit, notably in Romans 8:14-17.

A new access to God as Father

'All who are led by the Spirit of God are sons of God' (Rom 8:14).

One of the simplest definitions of Christianity is that it is a relationship with God. And it is true. When someone becomes a Christian there is a new sense of relating to God personally, of being led by the Spirit. The big change is that God is no longer distant or unreal. There is this strong sense of a living relationship. We are no longer separated from God by our sin. We are forgiven people. We are members of his family. We are sons and daughters of the living God. It is the essence of the covenant.

This is a rich and many-sided relationship. And consequently the New Testament uses a variety of different pictures to illustrate it, to illuminate this new and fulfilled way in which we relate to God through Jesus.

Christians are described as branches in a vine in John 15, as stones in a building in 1 Peter 2, as limbs of a body in 1 Corinthians 12, as soldiers in an army in 2 Timothy 2. They are all relational metaphors. They are pictures of belonging together, being part of the whole, and having a purpose as part of that wider identity.

But whereas these are pictures or metaphors designed to illuminate and fill out our understanding, the term 'sons of God' is the factual truth behind the metaphors. It is because we are sons of God in reality that we can now relate to God in these rich and varied ways. And it all depends on having access to God as Father.

Paul elaborates on the richness of this privilege. We have access to God as his children. God the Holy Spirit guides us in our lives. That in itself, as Paul explains earlier in Romans, is a direct result of what Jesus has achieved by his death and his resurrection: 'Through him we have obtained access to this grace in which we stand' (Rom 5:2). Paul carefully explains Jesus' role in making a way open, in making access to God possible.

The idea of standing in grace refers to a new and permanent position. It implies a security about our relationship to God. Once we were estranged. We stood as the objects of judgement before God. But, because of Jesus Christ's intervention on our behalf, God's attitude to us has now completely changed. We now stand in grace, not judgement. It means security. Circumstances now will never change. We have access to the Father as his sons and daughters for ever. And that access is secure because it has been obtained through Jesus himself. That is Paul's argument all the way through Romans up to the end of chapter 8.

Why is Jesus so significant in all this? Quite simply, Jesus has the exclusive right to make that access available. Kingdom rights are bestowed by the King himself. Only Jesus makes access possible, because only Jesus deals finally and completely with our sin.

That is what makes Christianity unique in all the world's religions. It offers forgiveness. A forgiveness paid for historically and completely by God's own Son. And this is the point from which the misconceptions about God's fatherhood usually spring. Some people fail to take into account that sin, our moral failures as human beings, prevents us from relating to a holy God.

Sin has to be paid for. Its effects are too drastic on the human and social levels, and above all on the spiritual level, to be casually overlooked. And it is only through Jesus Christ, who alone has the qualifications needed, that the relationship can be restored, and we can call God Father. That is why Christian privilege No 1 has to be a new access to God as Father. It provides a new way of relating to him, and a new experience of his strength and guidance.

A new assurance of acceptance by God as Father

'You did not receive the spirit of slavery to fall back into fear, but you have received the spirit of sonship' (Rom 8:15).

We all have fears of various kinds. Fear is a powerful psychological and spiritual factor in all of us. Fear affects our confidence, our direction, our motives, our ambitions, our relationships and many other issues. It can take on many different forms: we may be afraid of other people—of what they may think or say about us—we may be afraid of what might happen in the future, afraid of sickness or afraid of pain, afraid of death or dying. There is no shame in having fears. Everybody has them. It is how we handle our fears which really matters.

The New Testament emphasis is that *applied confidence* in the loving, caring fatherhood of God is the proper way to begin to handle these fears which can so easily depress us and render us ineffective in our lives.

He loves me—he loves me not. The most undermining, insidious and destructive fear for the Christian is a deep down feeling that we are somehow unacceptable to God, that we have no real right to be called his children. This comes back to lack of genuine assurance of salvation. And that has deeply undermining implications.

Without that assurance, we will inevitably lack confidence as Christians. Certainly, we become unable to apply that confidence to the pressure our anxieties exert upon us. The external fears of our lives begin to take control. We become spiritually timid. God's promises mean little in practice. Dryness rather than vitality and power characterizes the little prayer we are able to muster. And in our heart of hearts, it is possible to forget all about standing in grace. We begin to think of God not as a loving, forgiving Father, but as an angry, accusing judge.

Have we any right to be called God's children? The answer is 'Yes and no'. 'Yes', because of the promises of the gospel, but 'No', if we are looking to our own qualifications or religious efforts to achieve such a status.

In this respect, something subtle can happen. The temptation is always to be looking to ourselves rather than to Christ. Human beings have not changed. It has been the case for hundreds and hundreds of years. The psychological pressure to make ourselves acceptable to God is enormous. And it simply does not work.

Luther and the spiritual blues. In the beautiful city of Rome there is a strange building which stands opposite the Cathedral Church of St John Lateran. It is a rather unusual structure which houses the Scala Santa, the holy stairway. These are twenty-eight marble steps which were brought to Rome from Jerusalem by one of the earliest popes, and then erected into a shrine for the faithful.

The Scala Santa is the original authentic main stairway from Pontius Pilate's house. They are the steps which Jesus himself is said to have walked upon before he was taken to be crucified. So today they are an enormous attraction for pilgrims of various kinds, and have been for centuries past.

You can watch the pilgrims going up those steps on their knees, saying the rosary as they do. It has not changed since the days the young Martin Luther made his own celebrated pilgrimage to Rome. His story illustrates this whole question of assurance, and the fatal damage which can be done if this teaching is distorted.

The medieval church was a strange affair, not so different in some respects from the self-justifying world of the Pharisees of Jesus' time. Salvation had become a matter of trying as hard as you can, by all kinds of sometimes strange religious effort, to keep yourself out of purgatory. The medieval church had devised all kinds of wonderfully ingenious devices designed to clock up credit for the final reckoning.

In 1511 Luther was still an Augustinian monk. He had struggled for years genuinely to find acceptance with God. God was so holy, and Luther so sinful, where could poor Martin find rest for his troubled soul? His spiritual history of this period vividly portrays what horrifying misery he clearly went through.

With the opportunity to visit Rome for the first time, Luther took full advantage of all these old holy places in order to try to settle his spirit and find that elusive peace with God. It was a question of using to the full the best advantages Rome had to offer. The Scala Santa, the holy stairway, was the first attraction and was right at the top of his list.

With some anticipation, Luther made his pilgrimage to the Scala Santa. Like the other pilgrims, he began to climb Pilate's stairs in the footsteps of Jesus. Slowly and painstakingly he ascended on his hands and knees, following the rules as he went: the rosary in his hands, repeating the Lord's Prayer and kissing each step for good measure. He hoped by such a work of piety and merit, to deliver a soul from purgatory, and find peace for his own heart.

We have to remember this kind of desperate spirituality was real for people in those days, however ludicrous it sounds to us now. It is important to try to imagine the torment he went through.

The stairs were climbed, the Our Father repeated; the steps were kissed, the rosary completed. Luther had reached the summit of this medieval spiritual mountain. 'How can a man find peace with God?', that was his question. It had brought him to Rome. It had taken him to the top of the pilgrim's highest goal, the Scala Santa.

Luther tells us that at that very moment, on the very last step of Pilate's staircase, a personal miracle happened. Words from Paul's letter to the Romans came bursting into his mind and soul. He says it was like a piercing shaft of sunlight, illuminating everything which had been previously dark and gloomy. On the very top step—there on his knees, his head bowed down, the rosary clenched in his hand—these words from Romans penetrated his consciousness: 'The just shall live by faith.' They meant that forgiveness is free; it does not need to be earned, rather it is Jesus' gift from the cross.

Luther says he was absolutely bowled over. It appears he careered down those steps, apparently knocking over all the other pilgrims higgledy-piggledy as he went. And as he careered towards the bottom step, he proclaimed at the top of his voice: 'The just shall live by faith.'

It is said, perhaps with a tinge of enthusiastic exaggeration, that at that very moment the Reformation was born. Certainly the seeds were sown and Luther's life began to be changed. The church has never been the same since that Reformation of belief which Luther inaugurated. And it goes back to that moment of encounter with God—the day when Martin Luther found peace with God through the forgiveness of Jesus Christ.

From this point on, no longer did Luther think of God as an angry judge who had to be appeased by monumental human effort. God was now recognized as his loving, forgiving and merciful heavenly Father, because of faith in the sacrifice of Jesus Christ at Calvary.

Our acceptance by God today has not changed. It is on exactly the same basis. 'There is therefore no condemnation for those who are in Christ Jesus. For the law of the Spirit of life in Christ Jesus has set me free from the law of sin and death' (Rom 8:1).

The mumps and measles of the soul. Some Christians, like Martin Luther all those years ago, still live with a sense of constant condemnation. How should we respond to others or even ourselves when in that unhappy situation?

It is generally right to say that this sense of condemnation has far more to do with psychological feelings than spiritual fact. Our feelings are a notoriously unreliable guide to reality and Christian living. It is as well to be warned. Then our aim can be to believe in the promises of God, rather than to be thrown to and fro by the ups and downs of our emotions. Our feelings do need to be disciplined by truth. Otherwise truth will be undermined by our feelings.

Most people's feelings are like a sine curve. They have their peaks and their troughs—ups and downs which don't necessarily correspond to the reality of things at all.

The kind of person who wakes up early in the morning feeling gloomy and unworthy, who has a nasty attack of the spiritual blues, is well advised to meditate on the transforming statements of the Scriptures concerning forgiveness and fatherhood such as, 'The blood of Jesus cleanses [me] from all sin' (1 Jn 1:7) and, 'To all who received [Jesus], to those who believed in his name, he gave the right to become children of God' (Jn 1:12 NIV). The response should be: 'It is true. I am accepted. I am a child of God. I didn't have to contribute anything. He has done it all.' Every single failure and cause of shame has been dealt with. This is the kingdom reality. God would not be King at all if he were powerless to grant such freedom to his subjects.

A spiritual health warning. One of the subtlest tricks of the devil, when he finds himself unable to get at kingdom people via wine, women and song, is that he becomes religious. He loves to throw all our sins and failings at us and make us feel guilty. In Revelation the devil is described as the accuser of the brethren. We should expect him to live up to his name. He will accuse us by parading all our weaknesses and failings before us, as though they had never been forgiven by Jesus. And psychologically and spiritually we are poised very finely. Guilt is a major human problem, and Christians easily become subject to it.

We should be warned not to believe those annoying little messages in our head when we are feeling low. They are bad habits of mind which we need to deal with before they get the better of us. James' letter suggests some wise preventative measures: '"God opposes the

proud, but gives grace to the humble." Submit yourselves therefore to God. Resist the devil and he will flee
from you. Draw near to God and he will draw near to
you' (Jas 4:6-8).

If we have a low view of ourself, we can easily be
persuaded that we are not good enough to be used in
any way by God. But if we know we *are* children of God,
not only are our sins and failings and failures forgiven,
not only are we accepted, but God our Father wants,
indeed delights, to use us in his service.

Remember Paul's words: 'You did not receive the
spirit of slavery to fall back into fear, but you have
received the spirit of sonship' (Rom 8:15).

A new intimacy with God as Father

This is why we may enter boldly into the presence of our
heavenly Father: the Holy Spirit inspires a deep sense of
the intimacy of this new relationship. As Paul says:
'When we cry, "Abba! Father!" it is the Spirit himself
bearing witness with our spirit that we are children of
God' (Rom 8:15b-16).

The little word Abba is the distinctive name Jesus
used to address his heavenly Father. It is used by
Hebrew children to this day, and it means 'Daddy' or
'Dear Father'.

Most little children when they begin to speak make a
similar sound: Abba, Dadda, or Daddy. It is a child's
expression of recognition and trust. And when we begin
to recognize God as our heavenly Father, when the truth
of our relationship to him seeps all the way down to our
hearts, then the Spirit begins to inspire that deep sense
of recognition, trust and love that is natural to a child of
God. And in a spiritual sense, we do cry 'Abba! Father!'
Inwardly we recognize the love and stability of God as
Father.

It is a new intimacy with God which lends a sense of
warmth and closeness to the sometimes overwhelming
grandeur of the kingdom privilege. Every Christian has
this privilege to know God in this way.

A new inheritance from God the Father

Paul reserves the most staggering of his affirmations about sonship till the very last: 'We are children of God, and if children, then heirs, heirs of God and fellow heirs with Christ, provided we suffer with him in order that we may also be glorified with him' (Rom 8:16-17).

It is presented as a simple step of logic—a clear consequence of belonging: if we are children, then we are heirs. This is the language of inheritance. It speaks with tremendous power of a future hope which both touches and transmutes our experience of life in God and our day-by-day fellowship with Christ in this present order.

'My own little children,' Jesus said, 'it is your Father's good pleasure to give you the kingdom' (Lk 12:32). It is our inheritance because, as Paul says, we have been adopted; by grace we have been made sons and daughters of the living God. But as we shall examine further, along with this experience of glory for the present also belongs the experience of suffering. It is indeed a condition as Paul makes clear: '. . . provided we suffer with him in order that we may also be glorified with him.'

If the King did not escape suffering in this world, then neither can we. If, as the letter to the Hebrews makes plain, the King was made perfect by what he suffered, he will also prepare for the eternal kingdom through suffering those whom he has incorporated into his realm. 'For it was fitting that he, for whom and by whom all things exist, in bringing many sons to glory, should make the pioneer of their salvation perfect through suffering. For he who sanctifies and those who are sanctified have all one origin (Heb 2:10). Suffering and glory are themes of sonship and the kingdom which bring both reality and the tantalizing inner tension of the 'now and the not yet' firmly into view. They correct the expectations of those who have the supreme privilege of knowing God as Father. Those who inherit the kingdom as sons bear a family likeness to their fellow heir Jesus. They too will be glorified; they too will suffer.

The issue about whether God is the Father of all becomes so much more clear. It is in fact a privilege belonging only to the follower of Jesus Christ. It means a new access, a new assurance, a new intimacy, a new inheritance—knowing God, the Creator from whom we were once estranged, as Father and knowing the blessings of his kingdom, which are his right and joy alone to bestow.

> For all who are led by the Spirit of God are sons of God. For you did not receive the spirit of slavery to fall back into fear, but you have received the spirit of sonship. When we cry, 'Abba! Father!' it is the Spirit himself bearing witness with our spirit that we are children of God, and if children then heirs, heirs of God and fellow heirs with Christ, provided we suffer with him in order that we may also be glorified with him.

7

Communicating the Kingdom

Models for mission

The New Testament provides several mutually complementary patterns for communicating the gospel of the kingdom. They are models for mission. And in all these models, like the domestic art of baking a cake, method and ingredients stand together on a practically equal footing. It is always a matter of setting the ingredients and the method in complementary balance.

Of course when it comes to the task of evangelism there is never any foolproof recipe for instant success. What is our role? Our responsibility is solely to communicate the message accurately and effectively. It means using far more than just words alone; though words in themselves matter greatly, as the parable of the sower makes penetratingly clear. But it is God who changes people's hearts. He has supplied both the ingredients and the method. He will effect the changes and bring his subjects into his kingdom, if we will deliver the message.

Heralding the kingdom

Those who rightly emphasize the sovereign will of God

in these matters, have from time to time in history been guilty of underplaying the role of God's subjects in heralding the King's good news. Our part in all this, however, is an essential element used by him. He uses it in bringing people to a living faith in Jesus Christ. This emphasis is precisely what emerges from Peter's preaching on the day of Pentecost. It is the first example of public preaching in the life of the early church, and it has been recorded in some detail in Acts 2:14-36.

Peter—preaching about God

Peter's sermon on the day of Pentecost is one of the central models for mission of the New Testament. It provides a standard and lays down a pattern by which our own approach to communicating the kingdom today can be measured and directed.

There are five elements which make up both the ingredients and the method of this highly effective piece of gospel communication. They can be summarized as the visible, the prophetic, the personal, the historic, and the factual. To take proper account of this mission model, it will be instructive to analyse each one in turn.

The visible

> Peter, standing with the eleven, lifted up his voice and addressed them, 'Men of Judea and all who dwell in Jerusalem, let this be known to you, and give ear to my words. For these men are not drunk as you suppose, since it is only the third hour of the day.'
>
> (Acts 2:14-15)

In this way Peter begins his address to the crowd. A most notable feature of Luke's account is the emphasis placed on the fact that *Peter was preaching out of the visible context of changed lives*. This emphasis on the *visible* was a particular feature of the day of Pentecost. It was an extraordinary day. The Holy Spirit had given these disciples a supernatural ability to speak in other languages. Everybody heard the gospel in their own tongue. These are the same disciples who only a few weeks before had huddled together in an attic for fear of the Jews. They had been rendered totally ineffective, shattered by the crucifixion.

Here we see them remade by Pentecost. Their lives have been changed. So the scornful accusation of alcoholic intoxication—'But others mocking said, "They are filled with new wine"' (Acts 2:13)—is not so much to do with their Spirit-given ability to speak in tongues; it is far more to do with their Spirit-given joy. That is why the onlookers thought the disciples were tipsy. They were altogether different people. What had happened to the gloom? They were laughing. They were full of joy. Their dejection had been wiped away. They had been transformed as people.

Just as it is obvious that Peter's preaching rose from the context of changed lives, people today need to be able to see those changes in people who claim to be followers of Jesus today. Communicating the kingdom message is no use unless God is allowed to transform his messengers by letting the Holy Spirit do his work of sanctification and rebuilding. We have to communicate the kingdom out of the visible context of *our* changed lives. Only then will the gospel be taken seriously.

That transformation, which everybody could see, gave Peter his platform. 'Look at the changed lives,' he said. 'They are not drunk as you suppose. It is God who has done this. He has done the transformation.' And people will listen to us too, when we can show them that the truth has made a tremendous difference to our lives.

The method matters. It does not mean the fine details of organized evangelism—the debate as to whether rallies, door-knocking, evangelistic supper parties or whatever are the most effective or desirable style of evangelistic endeavour. Different cultures and areas have different needs. All these things are a matter of negotiation. But the method we see at work at Pentecost is different. The New Testament is not always prescriptive. In evangelism, it does not say, 'You *must* do this or do that . . . do it this way, do it that way.' But it is perfectly clear what you must *be*. It is straightforward. *Being precedes speaking*. We must be changed people.

We have already seen how the idea that we should be transformed if we are going to be the people of a King runs throughout the Scriptures. Why? Simply so that the message has integrity. That Peter spoke from the visible context of changed lives is a challenge to all of us to get our own witness and discipleship properly established—the integrity of the message depends upon the visible.

The prophetic

In Acts 2:17-21, 25-28 Peter quotes from Joel's prophecy and from Psalm 16, one of David's psalms. They are both passages of prophecy. But it would be inadequate to think that Peter was just providing a piece of Bible study for his Jewish listeners. There is more to it than that, even though the obvious way of communicating to Jews of this time was to expound the Scriptures to them.

What does the word 'prophetic' mean? Of the many things which could be said, prophecy certainly means the declaration of God, concerning what he has done, what he is doing and what he will do. The prophetic has a past, a present and a future. And prophecy is alive and real and active, because it is about God and what he does.

Peter is referring to the prophetic nature of this message, in its past, present and future aspects. In the past God had spoken through the prophet Joel, whom he now quotes:

> In the last days it shall be, God declares, that I will pour out my Spirit on all flesh, and your sons and your daughters shall prophesy, and your young men shall see visions, and your old men shall dream dreams; yea, and on my menservants and my maidservants in those days I will pour out my Spirit; and they shall prophesy.

> (Acts 2:17-18)

In effect Peter says, 'God spoke that in the past, but it is happening now. God has poured out his Spirit. No longer do you have to be a high priest or called to be a prophet to have a living knowledge of the Most High God. He has come to us. To all of us. Young and old. Male and female. The ordinary and the sophisticated. You can see the evidence in our lives. And this is the evidence promised in Scripture. What God declared would happen in the past, is now being fulfilled in the present.'

That covers the past and the present, but there is also a future dimension.

> And I will show wonders in the heavens above and signs on the earth beneath, blood, and fire, and vapour of smoke; the sun shall be turned into darkness and the moon into blood, before the day of the Lord comes, the great and manifest day. And it shall be that whoever calls on the name of the Lord shall be saved.
>
> (Acts 2:19-21)

The day of the Lord is the favourite term of the Old Testament prophets for the day of judgement. It is an event as yet still in the future.

In quoting this prophecy of Joel, Peter is clearly aware of the past, the present and the future of God's dealings with us. The good news of the kingdom is that for now anyone who calls on the name of the Lord shall be saved. It is set against that future reality of the day of the Lord, the day of judgement, when everyone will have to give an account of their lives before God.

Past, present and future intermingle. Gospel and kingdom intermingle. And their hope is present in the Old Testament, poised to unfold as God directs all human history to its goal and culmination in Christ. In Joel's prophecy, as quoted by Peter, such hope is made explicit. But it was not fulfilled till the coming of Jesus Christ. Today we must be sure in our own communication not to lose this prophetic sense of the message. God is active. His purposes are unfolding through history.

Where, then, should the emphasis in gospel communication be placed? Some today concentrate not on God and his purposes, but on man and his needs. Jesus will make you feel better, help you live longer, work harder. Jesus will make you happy, make you successful. Jesus will heal you, feed you, or whatever. Some of those may be true. But they are spin-offs. They are not the message itself. We have to recover this broad panoramic view of what God is doing in salvation: the unfolding of his purposes in history—past, present, and future. The message has to be directed to where any individual or group of individuals find themselves. But at the same time, the content of the message is prophetic. It is not primarily about man and his needs, though the gospel would not be good news if it did not ultimately fulfil all the needs of humankind. The essence of the message, however, is about God. And it is prophetic in its nature.

The personal

Jesus of Nazareth is the person of the message. When it is said that the message is prophetic, that it has a past, a present and a future, we are not speaking about an abstract philosophy. The message focuses in upon a person, Jesus of Nazareth. And it is instructive to see how Peter presents Jesus here as the person of this message.

> Men of Israel, hear these words: Jesus of Nazareth, a man attested to you by God with mighty works and wonders and signs which God did through him in your midst, as you yourselves know—this Jesus, delivered up according to the definite plan and foreknowledge of God, you crucified and killed by the hands of lawless men.
>
> (Acts 2:22-23)

As Peter says, 'God has made him both Lord and Christ, this Jesus whom you crucified' (v.36). But significantly, when he presents the message about Jesus to his hearers in verse 22 he is speaking about Jesus 'the man from Nazareth'. He is speaking of the man from that town in Galilee in the high valley in the southernmost hills of the Lebanon range. Jesus of *Nazareth*. Everybody knew his home town. Everybody knew what he had been doing publicly for the last three years. Everybody knew what his claims were. Everybody knew what had happened to him.

It is a very simple point. But people today in general do *not* know those things about Jesus. If the names Florence Nightingale, John F. Kennedy or Albert Einstein are mentioned, most people are able to say fairly easily what these figures are famous for. But it may not be quite so easy to report with accuracy both what they *said* on subjects particularly important to them, as well as giving some specific details about their lives.

This is certainly true of the average person's knowledge of Jesus today. We cannot assume they have any knowledge about him. Equally, many people do have quite wild misconceptions of what Jesus did say and do. So we should be clear that Peter presented Jesus the man. That is what he was—he was a man. There is no doubting his divinity, but his humanity was as complete as any other human being, except that he never gave in to the power of sin. Furthermore, Jesus' humanity is such a tremendously attractive presentation of God to us that, like Peter, we have to be careful to present this picture of Jesus the man rather than an unapproachable picture of divinity. The latter picture is closer to the docetic distortions of the second century than the attractive luminosity of the New Testament gospel figure.

But to be able to do this there has to be a continual absorption in all that Jesus said and did; a regular study of the gospels, getting to the root and the heart of Jesus' teaching. Then when we communicate this message we will focus in upon the man in such a way as to present the message as it really is, about Jesus.

Kingdom communication can be as dry as dust unless we are captivated by the person of the message. Instead it should be a combination of admiration, love, fascination, awe, gratitude and friendship. It comes from being absorbed in all the things Jesus said and did and what he has done for us.

Those who are captivated by him, without doubt communicate the good news of his love. But faith can slip back into a philosophy. Then it becomes lifeless.

Peter was talking about a person, not a system of ideas. The person of the message transforms lives.

The historical

'This Jesus God raised up, and of that we all are witnesses' (Acts 2:32).

There is an indispensable historical element to the message. When we talk to friends and contacts about the gospel, we are bound to encounter a whole variety of questions and responses, many of which will be perfectly reasonable. Some, of course, will be obstructive. But the majority of reactions are honest questions requiring honest answers.

There are, of course, some questions to which we simply do not know the answers—like any aspect of life —and it is best to admit that. But what comes out of this sermon of Peter's, and indeed from Paul's preaching elsewhere in Acts, is the *historical* nature of their message. They were asking people to come to terms with the evidence for the most unusual fact of history ever seriously recorded: that a man who had claimed to be God's own unique son, who was put to death by crucifixion for the crime of blasphemy, had come back to life again through being resurrected by a mighty act of God.

That is the historical nature of the message. Philosophers like Ludwig Wittgenstein, Bertrand Russell and A.J. Ayer can argue about the language of religion unendingly. But if the historical nature of the message is true, it does not matter what they say; they have to come to terms with the facts of history.

History will not go away. And that is why, along with Peter, Paul and the others, we today must always bring our friends back to consider the historical nature of the message. It saves going down many culs de sac. Everyone has to come to terms with the evidence and claims for Jesus's resurrection. Did it really happen? The evidence is that it did. And that kind of evidence simply cannot be ignored. Peter makes exactly the same assertion in his sermon. And it is exactly the same issue today.

The factual

'Let all the house of Israel therefore know assuredly that God has made him both Lord and Christ, this Jesus whom you crucified' (Acts 2:36).

Those are the facts. He is both Lord and Christ. All evangelism springs from that truth. That Jesus Christ is Lord and that he is God's Messiah is where our confidence springs from. As Peter says, we need to know it assuredly, because from beginning to end the message we are talking about is a message concerning the kingdom of God. It is a phenomenal reality concerning God's sovereignty, reign and rule over this world, both past, present and future.

God has put Jesus Christ into the ruling position over this world. He has made him Lord. From that position of complete supremacy Jesus now offers forgiveness, new life, the strength and power of the Holy Spirit to those who turn in repentance and faith to him. It is all about the rule, the kingdom of God.

So no one is going to defeat the purposes of Jesus Christ. Not the people we care for, who sometimes seem to have such powerful objections to faith in Christ; not the outright opponents of Christ and Christianity; not the massive powers of evil and destruction in the world today. Nothing is going to beat the purposes of the living God.

God has placed Jesus Christ into the supreme position. He is poised to return to this world. The day of the Lord will come. And when Christ returns he will bring in the fullness of his kingdom with him. It will be an end to war, an end to suffering, an end to pain and death, and an end to rebellion against God.

What difference does the supreme affirmation that God has made Jesus 'both Lord and Christ' make to your view of the world? What difference will it make to your confidence to take seriously the supremacy, the authority and the lordship of Christ? And what difference will it make to your concern for evangelism? What difference will it make as you share this message about

Jesus Christ—a message about what God has done, is doing and will do through him? How will it affect your perception of every opportunity you have before you, under the supreme lordship and direction of Christ, the Master of the universe?

These are the facts. As facts, they should affect our world-view, our confidence and our desire to share what is really best described as good news. He is Lord and Christ. Those two facts are meant to spur us forward into action.

Evangelism matters. It matters that our lives and our message reflect this model which God has given us. Ours is to be a transforming gospel proceeding from transformed lives.

The visible, the prophetic, the personal, the historical and the factual comprise both the ingredients and the method, but they are not a recipe for instant success. However, the five elements are integral parts of the truth which it is our responsibility to communicate faithfully and effectively.

Luke—communicating the truth

The question of a right approach for communicating the kingdom of God is something the New Testament does not shy away from. Luke the evangelist, for example, takes pains to examine closely and thoughtfully the whole issue of communicating gospel truth. This is particularly obvious when one examines the prologue to his gospels.

Inasmuch as many have undertaken to compile a narrative of the things which have been accomplished among us, just as they were delivered to us by those who from the beginning were eyewitnesses and ministers of the word, it seemed good to me also, having followed all things closely for some time past, to write an orderly account for you, most excellent Theophilus, that you may know the truth concerning the thing of which you have been informed.

(Luke 1:1-4)

Behind the scenes

Luke is the author of both the gospel which bears his name and the Acts of the Apostles. They are in a sense two volumes of the same work. This is clear from their dual dedication to Theophilus.

We can glean a reasonable amount of information about Luke. Supremely, Luke was a follower of Jesus Christ who was converted some time fairly soon after Pentecost.

Luke was certainly a Greek-speaker, though, in fact, racially speaking nobody knows whether he was a Jew or Gentile. He was a doctor, in the limited sense of medical knowledge of the first century. He was the friend and companion of the apostle Paul, who describes him as 'the beloved physician' in Colossians 4:14, and mentions him in several other places.

Luke is a very impressive figure. He was both an educated and cultured man; he was also a skilled and thoughtful historian. Because he had been a companion of Paul, he had worked in the forefront of the evangelistic strategy of the early church. But beyond all this, it is clear—both from his gospel as a whole and from these four verses of introduction in particular—that Luke's major gift was as a communicator of the first order. His overriding concern for effective communication is clear from the outset. We can see it from the dominant thought of the prologue to his gospel. He says he has assembled and presented all the facts about Jesus Christ. Why? 'That you may know the truth concerning the things of which you have been informed' (v.4).

He had a passion for communicating the truth. What can we learn from Luke the communicator, the author of Luke's gospel and the Acts of the Apostles, that will help us construct our model for mission today?

The authority of Luke's message

Luke says that many others had written about Jesus Christ: 'Many have undertaken to compile a narrative of the things which have been accomplished among us' (v.1). That word 'accomplished' refers, as what comes later makes clear, to the birth, life, teaching, death and resurrection of Jesus, and his subsequent ascension and pouring out of the Spirit on his disciples.

Many other narratives about these aspects of Jesus' life and teaching had been written before Luke began to research and compile his gospel. We can even date Luke's account, albeit roughly: from the absence of any reference to the Romans' destruction of Jerusalem, which happened in A.D. 70, we can assume that Luke's gospel predates that event. The sacking of Jerusalem was such a horrifying and significant event in terms of the Jews' national self-consciousness that it would surely have received a mention in Luke's gospel—or any other New Testament writing for that matter—had it been written *after* A.D. 70. The upshot of this is that Luke's gospel is an early document, probably dating from the late 60s of the first century and compiled during the lifetime of many of the foundational apostles of the early church.

It should not come as a surprise that many other people compiled narratives about Jesus. Of course this means more than just Matthew, Mark and John: there may have been hundreds of early documents or fragments about Jesus.

But of course it is natural that this would happen. Any famous figure who causes a stir tends to have a lot written about him, and it takes all kinds of forms. The question is whether what is written has any authority about it.

The Beatles have had literally millions of words written about them, yet there is still only one authorized biography which they claim represents the truth. Hunter Davies' book, which was originally written way back in 1968 and simply called *The Beatles*, is to this day, almost twenty years later, the only *authorized* biography among an immensely diverse library of articles, press reports and unauthorized books on the Beatles' lives and times.

How do you arrive at the truth—at whatever time in

history, and whoever your subject is—when there is a great deal of speculation and imagination about someone? The newspapers clearly demonstrate this dilemma.

Three of the most popular British tabloids were running major feature articles about Frank Bruno, the famous heavyweight boxer. The question really was: Who had it right? The articles all appeared on the same day with a similar claim. Their headlines were: 'Frank Bruno, the real story', 'Frank Bruno, the authorized story', 'Frank Bruno, the true story'.

They probably all added some embroidery to it. In fact Frank Bruno himself was obviously aware of the way reporters get things wrong, so he joined forces with Norman Giller, and produced an authorized biography called *Know what I mean?*

It is hardly surprising that there were many accounts circulating about Jesus Christ at the time Luke wrote his gospel. Major figures attract major attention. It was not so much that the other accounts were wrong, but Luke (as did Matthew, Mark and John) produced what is in some ways akin to an authorized biography. He wanted to set the record straight.

The authority for his gospel, as Luke says in verse 2 of his prologue, is vested in 'those who from the first were eyewitnesses and ministers of the word'. He went back to the original sources: the eyewitnesses. His was not fifth- or sixth- or seventh-hand information. It has come from those who were with Jesus during his lifetime, the disciples themselves.

Like Luke, if we are going to have anything to say about the kingdom to the world in which we live, we must be clear about the authority of our message. We must be clear about the facts. We must measure everything we say about God and his purposes for the world against the authentic and authoritative teaching of Jesus and the apostolic writers which we find in the gospels and the pages of the New Testament. The writers of the New Testament were either with Jesus themselves or in firsthand touch with those who were. Where else are we to get our truth?

Luke also points to the objectivity of his message. His first concern in presenting the truth to Theophilus was that there was a proper authoritative basis concerning, as he puts it, 'the things of which you have been informed'. It is objective: he has not made it up.

This very real concern for integrity and fidelity to the facts and the teaching of Jesus is immensely impressive when we consider that this almost scientific approach was completely unknown in the first century, except inside the small emergent Christian community. This is our authority too. We have nothing to say to our world, or to any of our friends or family, about Jesus Christ unless its authority reflects the teaching we have received from those who were with Jesus himself. We have no liberty to change their teaching. And if we depart from it we should not be surprised that people's lives are not in fact liberated, because God only blesses the truth. Like Luke, we must become students of the truth and immerse ourselves in its message.

The accuracy of Luke's reporting

'It seemed good to me also, having followed all things closely for some time past, to write an orderly account for you' (Lk 1:3).

For a considerable period of time, it appears that Luke dedicated himself to assembling an accurate picture of the teaching and the news about Jesus. Every single Christian today has the same responsibility of assembling as accurate a picture as possible of the teaching and news about Jesus; then, when there is opportunity to do so, we can present it to people in our own way.

Responding to opportunity

'Always be prepared to make a defence to any one who calls you to account for the hope that is in you' (1 Pet 3:15).

Peter's words present a normative command that is addressed to all Christians: we are exhorted to be properly prepared to explain our faith to anyone who gives us the chance to say something on the issue.

Controversy in the church which reaches the ears of the media often gives Christians important opportunities to say something clear and incisive for the kingdom. What do we say to a person when they repeat back to us some of the things they have heard from the media? When they show they genuinely cannot grasp the resurrection or the divine claims of Jesus, are we going to feel threatened and cross inside and blurt out bland statements of orthodoxy? Or will we prepare ourselves with all the facts and thoughts and arguments at our fingertips so that we can explain?

An accurate presentation of the facts—what happened, what was taught, and what we can be sure of—is irreplaceable if we are going to communicate effectively about Christ today. People have to be shown what the gospel means. And they have a right to have their questions answered. In so far as each of us is able, we must follow the model which we see in Luke himself: we must assemble the facts and make the picture clear.

The accessibility of Luke's language

'It seemed good to me . . . to write an orderly account for you' (Lk 1:3).

When Luke says he aimed to write an orderly account for Theophilus, we gain some considerable insight into his concerns for communication. The Greek word *kathexes*, translated 'orderly', probably does not mean strict chronological order. It much more implies that Luke wanted to present his message as a connected whole so that the complete and therefore undistorted picture about Jesus could be seen.

The accessibility of his language means that Luke is clear about the message he wants to put over. He presents that message as a coherent, connected, orderly whole. His language is subservient to that end. Luke's use of the Greek language is a model of clarity and effectiveness, he is the great stylist of the New Testament. He is a communicator.

There are several lessons for our attempts at

communication.

First, effective communication is not an ability the blessed few simply pluck out of the sky. Like so many other things in life, it is a case of 1% inspiration and 99% perspiration.

A concert pianist starts life practising scales. A boxing champion begins with a punching bag. There are hundreds of examples. The composer Brahms tore up every single thing he had ever written before the age of forty; he considered that only at forty was his apprenticeship as a composer complete. He concentrated thoroughly to get his communication right.

Effective communication, like any other skill, has to be practised: the more effortless and effective it seems, the more sure you can be that it will have taken hard work to achieve.

Are Christians particularly effective at communication? The mere presentation of bland orthodox statements about doctrine is not adequate. Doctrine is important, but there is far more to it than that. The way Christian leaders and others come over on the media is sad evidence that all is not well at this level of our responsibility. This highlights a tremendous weakness. On the whole, for some reason, Christians are not very good at communication. We have a terrific product, but we package it abysmally. It is no use just having the doctrine right. If we package up the truth in the clichés of orthodoxy, how do we expect the world around us to be intrigued, let alone gripped, by what we are saying?

The practice of communication

Like Luke, we should constantly be working on the accessibility of our language. Here are some practical suggestions.

The next time you have a discussion with a Christian friend, if it concerns a Christian issue, spend some time at the end talking about how you would explain that same issue to someone who is not a Christian.

Then, as you read the Bible day by day, spend some time working out what kind of language you would use to explain the passage to someone who has no Christian understanding at all.

If you read a daily newspaper, find one story each day to which you can make a Christian response. Then write out your view seeing if you can learn to communicate as clearly and effectively as the original newspaper story did, but in non-Christian language.

We will never improve if we do not work at it.

The priority of communication

The Holy Spirit can, and fortunately does, overrule in our communication. He so often gets through where we fail. But that must not be our get-out clause. God is concerned for communication. And he expects us to be too. We have to remember how staggering a fact it is to say, 'The Word became flesh.' The incarnation of Jesus as God is the biggest exercise in effective communication that history has yet seen. Effective communication is as important as right doctrine, prevailing prayer, holiness of life, and all the other imperatives of Christian living. Evangelism depends on it. It is an inescapable priority.

The other point to learn from Luke's communication is indeed to pray for the Lord to develop the effectiveness of our own communication. This should not just focus on the words we will use, but how we come over as total personalities. Remember, 'What we are speaks just as powerfully as what we say.'

Pray also for Christians who are professional communicators in broadcasting and the media. Particularly remember programme makers, researchers, presenters and writers. They are right in the front line. They have to be communicators of the first order. They need our prayers; they are in strategic situations and sometimes they are really up against genuine difficulties and opposition.

Another prayer target is to begin praying strategically for the emergence of another C.S. Lewis. Pray for the Lord to raise up another major Christian statesman of Lewis's stature who will be able, with integrity and accessibility, to speak to the world about Christ. In fact, we don't just need one, we need many such apologists. In our generation, on both sides of the Atlantic, there is a dearth of able Christian communicators who can speak on the same level as ordinary everyday people.

All these matters are genuine kingdom concerns, so they are close to the heart of God. Millions will listen to the gospel of the kingdom if we have apostolic authority in our message, if we present as a connected whole an accurate picture of Jesus and his teaching and if our language and persona are accessible to a non-Christian world.

The approach of Luke's ministry

'That you may know the truth concerning the things of which you have been informed' (Lk 1:4).

What was the approach, the purpose, the goal of Luke's ministry? It was to help another person to 'know the truth'. That is why this is a model for mission. It shows us our responsibility to help others appropriate the truth for themselves. It is not about knowing the truth intellectually on its own. It is about making the liberating truth of the gospel your own by taking hold of it. As Jesus said, 'You will know the truth, and the truth will make you free.'

If we aim to present the good news, this is it in essence: people from whatever background, in whatever turmoil, facing whatever crisis, can know freedom. And it is a freedom which comes from knowing and from taking hold of the truth about Jesus Christ which transforms lives.

Does that conviction burn in you? The word of God, the word of truth, changes people from deep down inside. This is God's way of doing it. And the work of evangelism consists in lining up our own efforts and approach in conformity with God's way of doing things as he has declared it objectively in his word.

This is what it means to communicate the kingdom, to have models for mission. Both Peter, who spoke about God at Pentecost, and Luke, who communicated the truth in a new written form, were major Christian communicators of their own time. They were men whose passion for truth was equalled only by their concern to communicate it. If God intends them to be our models for the kingdom, we really have to take on board their whole approach in order to become effective communicators of truth who speak about the eternal purposes of God the King. If ingredients and method form part of the same package, the provision of kingdom truth which changes people's lives must require that all followers of Jesus Christ today, for the sake of the kingdom, apply their lives and minds with dedication and vigour to working at getting the message over —whatever the cost—until the whole world hears and understands the transforming truth, power and purpose of the unfolding kingdom of God.

8

Kingdom People

'You are a chosen race, a royal priesthood, a holy nation, God's own people, that you may declare the wonderful deeds of him who called you out of the darkness into his marvellous light' (1 Pet 2:9).

A people with a purpose

The kingdom of God is a community concept. All through the New Testament it is made clear that those who are brought into the realm of salvation enter in as fellow members of God's family. The people of God are kingdom people because they derive their identity and direction in the world from Christ the King. He is guiding his people to the consummation of history, when he will return in divine power as both King and Judge, and as the bestower of eternal blessing for those who have given their full allegiance to him.

While God's people await the coming of their King, they are not passive. They are a people with a purpose. Corporately, they are to 'declare the wonderful deeds of him who called you out of darkness into his marvellous light'. In short, God's people are to be a *sign of the kingdom*. Just as Isaiah graphically prophesied the impact of the Messiah ('the people who walked in darkness have seen a great light'), so the people of God today are called to take on that same messianic role in openly declaring the saving deeds of the One who rescues from the realm of darkness and transfers to the kingdom of light.

Church and kingdom

With an explicit calling to identify with the role of the promised Messiah, what relationship do today's followers of Christ have to the kingdom of God? Is the church synonymous with the kingdom? Wherein lies the relationship?

The two biblical truths, church and kingdom, are part of the same whole; none the less, they are separate realities. Jesus made this clear by saying in the same breath, 'On this rock I will build my church,' while going on to speak of 'the keys of the kingdom' (Mt 16:18-19). In the same way, at the beginning of Acts, in the context of a question about the kingdom, Luke speaks in terms of the international ministry of the Holy Spirit spreading out from Jerusalem to 'Judea and Samaria and to the end of the earth' (Acts 1:6-8). Then, in the next chapter, he refers to the fellowship (*koinonia*) of believers, recording that day by day the Lord added new converts to the *church* (Acts 2:43-47).

Where, then, lies the distinction, and where the interrelationship, between the church and the kingdom?

The kingdom sums up all aspects of God's rule in the past, present *and* future dimensions of life. The church is the company of the redeemed; it comprises those who have drawn near to God, have made entry into his family and are ruled over by the King. However, while being sanctified by the indwelling Spirit, they are still to be perfected. When Christ returns, when the last trumpet sounds, we shall all be changed. But until then, the church has to struggle to become more like the full reality of the kingdom of God. God is at work among us. In our own integrity and devotion—our commitment to each other, our quality of life and, above all, our service to Christ—we must be a *sign* to the world of the rich reality of God's saving grace, power and love.

Everyone has a part to play. Indeed each person's part is essential because if we as the church are corporately to represent the kingdom of God to a world in darkness, then we have no choice but to pull together. And pulling together means having a clear vision of our reason for being. For without a biblical vision of what truly constitutes the people of God, the church becomes separated from the concerns of the kingdom, and the kingdom mission to powerfully and attractively commend the King becomes ingloriously thwarted.

Play your part

By consequence, a question Christians continually have to face involves the nature of what the church *is* and what it is meant to *be*.

It is clear from Paul's organic picture of the body in 1 Corinthians 12 that the church is designed to be an every-member ministry, where everyone contributes something of value by exercising their God-given gifts to the ministry of Christ's body as a whole. Paul underlines this in 1 Corinthians 12:27: 'You are the body of Christ and individually members of it.' He then goes on to describe different aspects of that body life in terms of mutual service and care, and the corporate life of the church.

From a casual reading of the New Testament, the dominant image of the body of Christ in the first century is of a church where everyone pulls together. Or is it? Was that the true situation? Did not Paul spend a great deal of effort in the Corinthian correspondence, as elsewhere, in *corrective* teaching? Was not the danger that lurked menacingly behind his words that followers of Christ, unchecked, can become passive? Then, as now, the church ran the risk of becoming a vehicle of passengers—a happy band, not of pilgrims but of spectators. Happy, that is, to let others do it all—to the severe detriment of the church's overall impact on the contemporary world and society in which Christ had placed his people for the sake of the kingdom.

We can read the Pauline correspondence through rose-coloured spectacles. All was not well in Corinth. And all is not well today. We are still repeating the old mistakes of the first-century Christians who, though they knew Christ, did not always live up that magnificently to his calling.

Paul's exhortation about unity

Like kingdom and church, service and commitment belong together. The church cannot be a sign of the kingdom if the very essence of the church's organic identity as the body of Christ is ignored in practice. To separate what God has joined together spells trouble for the people of God. This concern accounts for the special emphasis Paul gives to this issue in several places, most notably towards the end of the letter to the Romans: 'I appeal to you therefore, brethren, by the mercies of God, to present your bodies as a living sacrifice, holy and acceptable to God, which is your spiritual worship' (Rom 12:1).

As befits his background and education, Paul uses words with extreme care, so that every word and phrase counts with precision in what he wants to say. It is instructive, therefore, to analyse both the way Paul presents his argument, the tone of what he is saying, and the argument itself, i.e. the subject-matter of what he wishes to communicate.

There are three separate aspects to note about the manner of Paul's presentation of his concerns. And they are all present in the phrase, 'I appeal to you therefore, brethren, by the mercies of God . . . .'

The weight of Paul's words

'I appeal to you,' says Paul.

The pop musician, Bob Geldof, is a household name on both sides of the Atlantic. As well as being a leading figure in the pop music business, he has become most celebrated for his work in fund raising for famine relief.

The international, world-wide Live Aid broadcast of 1985 raised a tremendous amount of money for Ethiopia, as did several subsequent appeals for other stricken areas of the world.

One of the most striking aspects about Bob Geldof is the passion, intensity and conviction with which he comes over as a person. One example illustrates that intensity with particular vividness.

There was a deeply moving moment during the broadcast, when at one point, suddenly and without warning—in front of the cameras and many millions of viewers—Bob Geldof crashed his fist down on to the table with tremendous ferocity. With unusual conviction and passion, he said directly to the audience, 'We want your money. Give us your money right now. There are people dying out there at this very moment.' There was an enormous conviction, concern, determination and weight to his words. In view of the terrible scenes of death, poverty, disease and deprivation which television viewers had been witnessing for some weeks, it was almost as disquieting as it was moving.

When Paul says, 'I appeal to you,' he is equally passionate in his concern. He is using a very strong expression in Greek. It is the word *parakaleo*. It means 'I beseech you' or 'I beg you'. The same Greek word is used in Mark 1:40, when the leper beseeched Jesus to heal him: '[The leper] came and knelt in front of [Jesus] and begged to be healed' (Living Bible). *Parakaleo* is a very strong and weighty expression. Paul was making a passionate appeal.

The addressees of Paul's words

'I appeal to you therefore, brethren . . .' The 'you' is plural. It is easy to miss the fact that Paul's appeal is corporate. Paul is addressing the brethren, the whole church, not just isolated individuals.

This is an appeal, not simply to an individual, to tighten up his performance; it is a passionate and committed appeal to the whole church to pull its efforts for Christ into shape. Each member of a church has a part to play. This is why Paul chooses his words so carefully. He does not want any member to be in doubt. The word *brethren* is an instance of this.

Brethren may sound a little old fashioned today but it means something specific. It means that real Christians are brothers and sisters in Christ. It means we are members of a family we have been given a deep bond of belonging together.

If that is genuinely true, then there is a question to face. Will we take seriously the fact that we have this bond of belonging together? And therefore does the church —the real church, the family of believers—really matter to us? Or are we spiritual isolationists, only interested in individual Christianity and willing only to be spectators?

Paul's appeal is plural because for him the church really does matter. Furthermore, he is clear that each individual is responsible for the health of the whole. We cannot escape that equation. Sad to tell, the powerless churches are the ones in which people duck out of their corporate responsibility. The churches which really hum with life and effectiveness are where every member is properly involved and used in God's service.

The theology of Paul's words

'I appeal to you therefore, brethren, by the *mercies of God* . . . .'

In any household with young children, breakfast time can often be a combination of high comedy and passionate struggles actually to get the breakfast consumed, rather than having it projected missile-like all over the kitchen. It has certainly been the case with our young family of two little girls.

Halfway through breakfast one memorable morning, Rebecca, then two years old, suddenly decided she did not want any more of her Rice Krispies. She obviously preferred the look of her father's toast and marmalade instead. There was no reason why she should not have had some of the toast, except she had only eaten two spoonfuls of cereal thus far.

After failing miserably to persuade her to eat up, I tried an appeal. Instead of saying, as I normally do, 'Go on Rebecca eat it up . . .', I thought I would appeal to her better nature, so for the first time I tried, 'Come on Rebecca—*do it for Daddy.*'

There was a moment's silence. The cereal was contemplated thoughtfully. Then, in Rebecca's best baby-speak, out came the words, 'For Daddy.' And in went the Rice Krispies, just like magic. I was amazed. The appeal worked.

When we make an appeal, we are asking for a response. A response can be to someone or to some thing; whichever it is, we are asking that pure self-interest be set aside, and that the interests of the object of the appeal should take precedence.

Within the limits of our fallenness as creatures, we all learn from a very early age that pure self-interest can be set aside, and a response can be made to another or higher interest. The higher interest in this case being 'Do it for Daddy.'

This illustrates the basis, the theology, of Paul's plea. He appeals to a higher interest. Paul appeals by the mercies of God.

What is he appealing *for*? What he wants is the real involvement of every member of the church. But it is not to be on the basis of pleasing yourself, nor to please the rector, minister, elder, or whoever; it should be to pleasing God alone. As such, it is to be a theological response—a response to the mercies of God.

The mercies of God is a revealing phrase. Why does Paul choose this particular expression?

Clearly, those who serve God with dedication deeply value their salvation through Christ. Yet it is equally obvious that those who have little concern for dedicated service, have scant understanding of the value or the cost of what Jesus has done for them.

It is like that because, for Christian service to have any lasting value, it has to be a response to the mercies of God. Otherwise it is not service, it is something else. We can call it good works, charity—whatever we like—but it is not service.

'I appeal to you therefore, brethren, by the mercies of God.'

In that short sentence we see the *manner* of Paul's appeal and the weight of the words. We also see to whom those words are addressed, as well as the theology underlying them. With our increased perception of Paul's approach, we can now enter in more fully to the *content* of his appeal.

Paul's priorities

Get the attitude right

'I appeal to you . . . to present your bodies . . . .'

That phrase means 'offer yourselves'. We have to get the attitude right if we want to properly involve people in the church.

It is no good either cajoling people into service or entering into service ourselves as though we are doing someone a favour. We have to be willing to serve and willing to offer ourselves. We must be willing without wanting to add wrong kinds of preconditions.

I was impressed by someone I met coming in our front door one day; he had turned up to lend a hand when we were moving house. What he did was very ordinary, but it was his simple willingness that impressed me. As soon as he came in, he took off his jacket and just said, 'Here I am. What can I do?' That is the attitude for Christian service, being willing, being available—offering yourself and being prepared to serve.

Sometimes we may not automatically feel we have that attitude. But feelings *can* come second. We can work on the attitudes even though, perhaps, we are not overwhelmed with enthusiasm for a project. We are always going to be battling with self-centredness, but that is one of the reasons God has given us Christian service. It is a means of grace. It is to help us overcome our natural self-centredness.

Attitudes can be worked on. But decisions have to

be made some time. We may have to decide to be involved, to offer ourselves and to serve God.

Get the standard right

'I appeal to you therefore, brethren, by the mercies of God, to present your bodies as a *living sacrifice*.'

If Christian service is not truly sacrificial, it is not in honesty worth very much. This is why Paul chooses these words so carefully. He asks us to offer ourselves as a living sacrifice.

The standard must be right. Sacrifice is called for. If we are to serve God, we will have to make sacrifices of some kind or other. It is best to enter in with our eyes open. In the end, of course, such sacrifice brings about a very deep liberty. But to start off with, you have to be clear about the standard. It has a great deal to do with sacrifice.

Get the values right

'I appeal to you . . . to present your bodies as a living sacrifice, *holy and acceptable to God*.'

Christian service always has a moral dimension to it—as well as a practical one. Part of sacrificial service is sacrificial living. In an important sense, it is a quest for *holiness* in order for our lives to be properly consecrated to God.

These values matter in the spiritual realm. Holiness is something to take seriously. But perspectives matter too. None of us has to be a super-saint. It is a willingness to live to please God alone which really matters. As Paul says, this is what God finds acceptable. It is the willingness which counts.

There is no one who is not good enough to serve. If any of us feels we are an under-achiever spiritually, we should not let that hold us back from Christian service. It is not what we have achieved so far which matters, but how dedicated we are prepared to be for the future. It is indeed simply about willingness.

Get the heart right

'[All this] is your spiritual worship.'

Has it ever struck you that Christian service is in essence a form of worship? The idea of worship in the New Testament has several different facets; sadly, we tend today to limit the use of the word *worship* exclusively to what we do in church on Sunday.

What is true spiritual worship? According to Paul it is an attitude of the heart towards God. It is an attitude of worship to want to please him. In saying that, we have come full circle; we are back to the idea of response to the mercies of God. Real worship is a response of gratitude; and that response can take many forms.

If we really want to worship God, we will serve him. And we will serve him not only in our job or our studies or our home or our community, we will also serve him, in some way, in the church. That is God's will for us. He has made it explicitly clear in his word.

All Christians, from whatever background, need to get their thinking about worship straight. It is no good singing hymns and choruses, reading the Bible, praying, and thinking that in doing these things we are worshipping God. We have to serve God both inside *and* outside the church. That, according to Paul, is our spiritual worship.

In the end, it all has to come from our heart. It is a subtle but important balance, and it makes the essential difference. We have to put the object of Christian service into perspective. It must be clear. We are not serving the church, we are serving the Lord. That balance matters. And unless we serve him with love, it will be of doubtful spiritual value. By contrast, if we are concerned to worship God by what we do out of sheer devotion to him, what a real difference that will make!

The church is meant to be an every-member ministry. But lazy Christians have the effect of stifling the work of the Holy Spirit. Consequently the church becomes ineffective. The ministry of any church—and remember the church is designed to be an effective sign of the kingdom—will not become truly effective unless each of us plays our part, singly and together. That is why Paul appeals so passionately. The stakes are set so high. This is also why we must not shirk the application. Will I get involved? Will I serve Christ from my heart? Will I help pull together? It *does* matter. The impact of the church, for the gospel and the kingdom, depends on it.

Paul makes a passionate appeal for committed involvement. He desires that church and kingdom should be one in purpose and identity. He wants every member to play their part: 'I appeal to you therefore, brethren, by the mercies of God, to present your bodies as a living sacrifice, holy and acceptable to God, which is your spiritual worship.'

Facing opposition

'Blessed are those who are persecuted for righteousness' sake, for theirs is the kingdom of heaven' (Mt 5:10).

Jesus linked the experience of service with the fact of opposition. In a curious way, when opposition is encountered it is a sure sign of membership of the kingdom. If the King himself did not escape persecution, then neither will his subjects. That is a constant New Testament theme. Yet Christians often become half-hearted in their service; they are often tempted to give up altogether. Why is that? Mainly because they have received inadequate preparation for the opposition which kingdom people inevitably meet if they set out to serve Christ in the world.

Paul's first letter to the Thessalonians offers some considerable insight into what it means to suffer opposition for the sake of the kingdom. In the first part of 1 Thessalonians 2, Paul's specific response to some of the issues of opposition clarifies what is to be the proper reaction of kingdom people to such apparent hurdles.

First, however, we need to sketch in some of the background to this situation; that will then illuminate the particular edge and forcefulness of Paul's radical and impassioned approach.

At the time of writing, Thessalonica was the capital city of Macedonia, which in turn was a Roman province. Today, it is part of northern Greece. And Thessaloniki, as it is now known, is still a flourishing and important city. It is the government and administrative centre for that northern part of Greece and second only in importance to Athens itself.

1 Thessalonians was written around or just after A.D. 50. This was at about the time when Paul, along with Silas and Timothy, embarked upon their second missionary journey. The church at Thessalonica was founded by Paul during that journey and precise background details are recorded by Luke in the first part of Acts 17.

Paul experienced unusually forceful opposition at this time. There was tremendous antagonism from the Jews in particular. The synagogue community did not at all like the new teaching of Paul and his friends. The vocal element within this particular Jewish group were highly intolerant of Paul's teaching in all its aspects—including what he said about Christ, about Jesus' sacrifice on the cross, and about his resurrection. They made a great deal of trouble. Acts 17:5 describes it vividly.

The Jews were so jealous of Paul and his preaching that they rounded up the local thugs, formed a mob and started a riot in the city. On top of that, the Jewish opposition then heaped all the blame for the riot on Paul and the Christians, claiming quite dishonestly to the authorities that Paul was proclaiming Jesus as a new king over Caesar.

Paul's mission to Thessalonica created some significant antagonism. The Jewish opposition was physically violent, intolerant and abusive. The Jews had stirred up mob violence in a big city, and the situation had grown very hot indeed.

As a consequence, Paul and his companions did not stay long in Thessalonica. But the foundations they laid did take root, and the church began to grow very effectively in numbers and in quality. So what happened to that initial opposition?

The physical violence of opposition came to an end but the intolerance and abuse did not. The new tactic of the opposition was to conduct a whispering campaign. This was a campaign against Paul himself, undermining his integrity and denying his message. It was designed to unsettle the allegiance of those who had given their lives to Jesus Christ through hearing Paul's message. It was a smear campaign; and it was, it appears, quite unpleasant.

Public figures—from cricketers to pop stars—often attract this kind of attack and Christians are in no way immune.

The mud-slinging at Thessalonica was clearly directed at the apostle Paul. The Macedonian press was full of stories about him in their gossip columns. The local Thessalonian papers featured violently defamatory articles about him on their front pages. It was a carefully orchestrated smear campaign. The whispers had grown into a roar of bitter character assassination. The aim? That was simple: they wanted to undermine Paul's message; they wanted to show up Paul's teaching as bogus—to prove him a fraud and a liar.

Our knowledge of the venomous attack that Paul faced in Thessalonica illuminates with force the truth behind Jesus' warning concerning opposition. No one is immune, all must be prepared. Paul's reaction to the vilification and attack he received also assists us today in assessing and applying to our own lives and situations the genuinely radical principles which lie behind Paul's thoughtful and measured response to this unsettling experience of opposition which he faced.

Motives and methods

1 Thessalonians 2:1-12 contains Paul's response to these accusations. Here he sets out his rebuttal of the whispering campaign which had been conducted against him. The reason Paul commits himself to print is because the campaign had been unsettling the faith and witness of the Thessalonian Christians and he wants to reassure them of his motives and his methods—they need to be

assured of the validity of the message they received and believed.

Paul's main concern is the issue of how to combat opposition. He mentions three major elements of *response* to opposition and five briefer elements to do with example when *facing* opposition. The principles at work in this letter speak directly to us today as we ourselves encounter opposition.

How will all this apply to us? We may not necessarily be public figures. But we all face opposition of some kind or other as Christians. The world around us has a different set of values. There is, and has always been, a built-in dislike for much of what Christians stand for. Jesus made it clear from the outset that kingdom people will always face opposition. The real question is to do with *reaction*: Just how should the kingdom people of God react when facing up to opposition?

Paul's courage in God. 'For you yourselves know, brethren, that our visit to you was not in vain; but though we had already suffered and been shamefully treated at Philippi, as you know, we had courage in our God to declare to you the gospel of God in the face of great opposition' (1 Thess 2:1-2).

How do you react when the pressure mounts? Are you the kind of person who battles on? Or are you the person who wilts in the heat? We are all different: constitutionally, some of us do seem to sink under pressure while others of us naturally seem to be survivors.

As far as Paul is concerned it really does not matter how we are constituted, whether we are *naturally* a winner or a loser; it is the difference made by being in Christ which matters. The issue for Paul is to have courage in God. The language he uses here in the Greek text is illuminating. The word Paul uses for having courage in God, is the Greek expression *parrhesiazomai*. It means a kind of boldness—a boldness based upon precedent and on lessons learnt from the past. Furthermore, it opens up an aspect of faith in an illuminating way.

When our daughter Rebecca caught chicken pox at

the age of two and a half, I had only recently recovered from it myself. She had observed my recovery with interest, and took it on herself to learn an important lesson from my experience. As parents we had not prompted her. During the time of *her* illness, when we or anyone else asked Rebecca about her chicken pox and how she was feeling, she had one standard, confident reply: 'My spots will get better.' That is all she said. And she said it every single day for two weeks, whenever anybody asked her. She was right. They did get better!

Sometimes children are much better at learning the lessons, the basic truths about life, than us adults. They learn the lessons more quickly, and they remember them. Spots do get better. Rebecca's confidence was based upon the simple lesson she had learnt from seeing my own spots disappear. And it gave her courage. If Daddy's great big spots could get better, then so could Becky's.

Learning our lessons is the only really dependable basis for courage and boldness. We have to take hold of the lessons we have learnt in the past, and apply them to the present. And this applies especially in the spiritual realm.

Why did Paul have this courage and boldness in God? Well, he had seen God prove his power so many times before. He had learnt the lessons of the past, and he applied those lessons to this present situation. This is why he could direct the Thessalonians back to the past, to think again about the outcome of his mission to Thessalonica. Have they learnt the lesson?

He says, 'Our visit to you was not in vain.' He directs their gaze backwards. There is the church, steaming ahead now. The mission was no failure. God did it. God does not fail. Because of the lessons he learnt in the past, his courage in God gave him boldness to declare the gospel in the face of opposition.

There is no strength for us in the present, unless we learn the spiritual lessons which God has taught us from our past. That is why Israel had its festivals. That is why we Christians have Christmas and Easter, baptism and the Lord's Supper. They help us to learn the lessons of the past. They are great reminders of the ways in which God has revealed his utter dependability to us. But there are other lessons, personal lessons, we also need to learn.

It is of such value to look back in a personal way and review what God has done for us. This was the constant practice of the psalmist. The backward gaze strengthens us to trust in someone who does not change—someone who can be trusted in all circumstances, even when the going becomes difficult.

What kind of lessons from the past do you need to learn about God? Are there lessons God has taught you, but which you have not really heeded? Is your memory getting a little short?

It does not matter what kind of person we may be naturally. Some sink under pressure; some are naturally fighters. What we really need to be is a learner. We need to learn objectively from what Jesus has done on the cross and through the resurrection, and we need to learn personally from what he has done in our own lives and the lives of others. Then we can have that kind of boldness, that courage in God, which will carry us through when the going becomes difficult and uphill and we are in the midst of opposition. If we have never faced opposition, it certainly will come in some form or other. That is why we need to learn the lessons now. It is the basis of Paul's courage in God.

Paul's confidence in his calling. 'For our appeal does nor spring from error or uncleanness, nor is it made with guile; but just as we have been approved by God to be entrusted with the gospel, so we speak' (1 Thess 2:3-4).

Political debates, as we see them relayed and reported through the media, are not always particularly worthy affairs. Different positions on issues are often out-matched by the strenuous efforts employed to under-mine each other's arguments. In fact it is the classic method of confrontational politics. It aims to under-mine not only the arguments but also the personal *character* of the political opponent.

Leaders of all parties seem to be very skilled at this. Demolish the man or woman first and the chances are you will bring their message into disrepute because you are undermining motives or competence or both. That, at least, is the theory.

Paul faced this kind of opposition. Not only for his message, but also as a person, he was coming under fire. Paul was being written off by the antagonized and outraged members of the synagogue.

His response? 'We speak as men approved by God' (1 Thess 2:4 NIV). Paul had confidence in his calling.

Confidence in our calling makes all the difference. We should not be surprised that people see things differently to us. There will always be opposition and we should not be surprised. But when we face opposition, the important factor is to remember our calling. Why? Because we belong to God for ever. And we must remember that he has called us to the specific situation we are in at the moment. If Paul could face intolerable abuse and vilification at Thessalonica, yet still recognize his calling to be valid in that very place, so can we—wherever we are.

This means that wherever we are situated—no matter what the opposition—we are in the right place to do things for God: in an office where there is a manager who plays plain unfair; in a family where one member's behaviour—husband, wife, parent, or whoever—has become a deep burden to us; in a flat where one of the people we share with is being so difficult—wherever we are, we are in the right place to do things for God, and to see these pressures as potential opportunities.

We should and can have confidence in our calling. Opposition, discomfort and difficult times all provide opportunities in which God can act, just as he acted through Paul in Thessalonica. His experience is an object-lesson for us. Look at what was achieved there, *in the face of opposition*. When the going becomes a struggle there are the opportunities for God to act. It is human to feel the pressure; but it is immature to run away.

Paul's concern to honour God, not man. 'So we speak, not

to please men, but to please God who tests our hearts' (1 Thess 2:4b).

One of the ways we set limits to our effectiveness as Christians is when we become too concerned about our reputations, when we worry too much about how we come over to others and how they see us. Our self-image becomes paramount, so we concentrate on the way our self-image governs what we let other people see of us. Much of our behaviour is constrained by how we like other people to see us and we work very hard at controlling their image of us.

Do you have a gap between how you see yourself—your self-image—and the way you want others to see you—the image you try to project to other people? It is a subtle fact about our human nature which we have to come to terms with if we want to be effective servants of Christ in this world.

It does not have to be skeletons in the cupboard which we are trying to hide—though some do have those still-undealt-with things lurking away in the background. But everyone has something to keep away from public view, something they do not like or which they find unacceptable about themselves. But, unfortunately, that kind of attitude ends up eroding our effectiveness.

One problem is to do with the energy it uses up. We can spend so much effort worrying about the way we come over to others, that we can make ourselves ineffective spiritually. Sometimes it is a failure to let the gospel go deep into our lives, a failure to see how deeply God loves us, how completely he accepts us and how thoroughly he forgives us. But he will deal with our skeletons if we let him. And when we genuinely let him transform us, how powerfully that works in our witness to others.

God wants us to be transparent people. There should be no difference between the outside and the inside. We should behave no differently in private than in public.

Transparency is a wonderful Christian quality, and a powerful Christian witness. Again it is all part of the church living up to its calling, and being a sign of the kingdom. How will people believe our message that Jesus Christ transforms lives, unless we ourselves are transformed? And that transformation has to become transparently visible for the kingdom to break through the sometimes sadly valid cynical criticisms levelled against the church by the outside world concerning its integrity and vitality.

No one becomes an angel overnight. But I can think of Christian people who, because they have let the work of Christ go deep into their lives, appear to wear no mask at all. There is no gap between the private and the public. Nothing is hidden. The skeletons have been thrown out of the cupboard. It is letting the truth of the gospel sink deep into us which achieves this.

This kind of transparency of character is not beyond any one of us. Transparency comes from the desire to honour God, and not be over-concerned for our own reputation.

Do you know how all these inner conflicts and turmoil of ours can be dealt with? It is when we give up pandering to them. Do not let your self-image be the back-seat driver of your life: 'Do this, do that. Go this way. Go that . . .' When we start putting God first and honouring him, we will overcome the stranglehold which our image of our self so powerfully exerts upon our life. And then we will become truly effective for God.

In Thessalonica, in a situation of potentially deep discouragement, Paul broke through—and his responses should spur us on too. We need, today, that same courage in God—and we need to be prepared to learn from the past. We need, today, that same confidence in our calling. We need, today, that same concern to honour God.

So often it is the uncomfortable situations which are opportunities for God to act, when we learn about courage, confidence and concern to honour God, then there will be consequences—consequences to do with the effectiveness of our ministry to others.

Five consequences

Having outlined the three elements that go to make up a Christian response to opposition, Paul sets out five consequences concerning his example when facing opposition—consequences which involve the effectiveness of our ministry to others.

Paul's manner. 'We were gentle among you, like a nurse taking care of her children' (1 Thess 2:7). Note the gentleness of manner, and the love it implies.

Paul's openness. 'Being affectionately desirous of you, we were ready to share with you not only the gospel of God but also our own selves, because you had become very dear to us' (1 Thess 2:8). Note the openness of life. Paul was prepared to share himself as part of his ministry.

Paul's commitment. 'For you remember our labour and toil, brethren, we worked night and day . . .' (1 Thess 2:9). What can we learn from that quality of persistence and commitment? Is there something requiring more of an effort, a deeper dedication, for God?

Paul's purity. 'You are witnesses, and God also, how holy, righteous and blameless was our behaviour to you believers' (1 Thess 2:10). There is that transparency again. Who does not need to work on this? Purity and transparency are such important elements in our witness and communication to others.

Paul's goal. 'We exhorted each one of you and encouraged you and charged you, to lead a life worthy of God, who calls you into his own kingdom and glory' (1 Thess 2:11-12). There is the vision—a vision of lives lived to the glory of God and for the sake of the establishment of his kingdom. It is in fact the goal against which to measure any vision we have for living out the Christian life.

Learning the lessons

Opposition is the practical consequence of living a life dedicated to the kingdom of God. How do we face opposition? By exercising courage in God. By having confidence in God's calling. By being concerned to

honour God, and not men. This is the way to respond
when you are living in the face of opposition.

Opposition in one form or another is all around us.
Opposition will either knock us out of the ring altogether or it will succeed wonderfully in sharpening the
effectiveness of our life and service. Christians today
face tremendous pressures. It is when we are up against
it that our standards are most likely to slip. That is the
point of smear campaigns, character assassinations, and
the quieter undermining of our confidence by stupid
jokes, comments and insinuations.

Unfair treatment and opposition can take many
forms. Paul spoke about the opposition he faced in
Thessalonica because he wanted the Christians there to
learn the same lessons he had learnt. And they are the
same lessons we also must learn today.

We can and should have courage in God. It affects
our boldness. We must learn the lessons of the past and,
in particular, the personal lessons which God has taught
us.

We can and should have confidence in our calling. We
belong to God. Where we are is where God has led us to
be. Until he moves us on, this is the place of opportunity
and not somewhere else.

We can and should be concerned to honour God and
not men. It is of first importance that we redirect the
concerns of our lives spiritually towards God. How
many of us waste valuable spiritual energy pandering to
the commands and desires of our own self-image? Do
you need to do some work on inner purity, self-accept-
ance and putting God first at the levels of your life
where it really matters?

How can I best glorify and honour God in all that I
do? If we make God our goal, then many of our inner
struggles will simply slip into place. When we have set
ourselves to glorify God, we can aim, like Paul, at these
qualities: gentleness in our manner, openness in our
lifestyle, commitment to God's work, and purity in our
motives.

This is what Paul learnt in times of very tough opposition. It is for the tough times in whatever form they may take that we are in training to fulfil our calling as kingdom people.

The kingdom of God needs people who are courageous, confident and transparent in the service of God. We need not be discouraged, for none of us is born like this; but every one of us can change by the grace of God. That is the transforming work of Christ through the Spirit within us. It is the gospel. But our response and co-operation are required. We will change when we have, along with Paul, this goal above all: 'To lead a life worthy of God, who calls you into his own kingdom and glory' (1 Thess 2:12).

9

Kingdom Responsibilities

'You cannot serve both God and money' (Lk 16:13 NIV).

Jesus said it is impossible to serve both God and money. It would be like a servant attempting to serve two masters. 'Either he will hate the one and love the other, or he will be devoted to the one and despise the other' (Lk 16:13 NIV). Jesus made these observations while speaking of the new era where the kingdom of God has entered into its mode of fulfilment. 'The Law and the Prophets were proclaimed until John. Since that time, the good news of the kingdom of God is being preached, and everyone is forcing his way into it' (Lk 16:16 NIV).

Revolution and repentance

Mention the kingdom of God in the turbulent, hotheaded times in which Jesus lived, and the political temperature rose immediately. Revolution rather than repentance was the conditioned reflex of thought among the oppressed, passionately nationalistic Jews of the first century—living, as they did, under the cruel, unfeeling ways of Rome and Caesar. The Zealots wanted to force the issue. The rule of God could be brought in by revolution and violence, so they claimed.

Yet Jesus was just as radical. In fact his radicalism goes far deeper than any of the freedom fighters of his time, though only his followers properly appreciated the particular nature of the revolution in the soul of man which Jesus was inaugurating; and they too only grasped its full significance after the resurrection, when Jesus spent forty days speaking to them and teaching them about the kingdom of God.

Jesus' teaching was radical and revolutionary because it made and continues to make a requirement of repentance. As Luke makes clear, Jesus said that when the kingdom of God is preached, the good news requires a response every bit as forceful, determined and radical as that urged by those with whom his hearers were so familiar—those who would seek to achieve their results by sheer force of arms.

Repentance and not political revolution is the proper response to the kingdom. God requires of us a fundamental reworking of our allegiances in life. For when we take up privileges as the kingdom people of God, we also take on responsibilities. Whatever was our attitude before becoming incorporated into God's eternal plan for the kingly rule of Christ, now we are God's people we must share the concerns of the King for the world. 'He has showed you, O man, what is good. And what does the Lord require of you? To act justly and to love mercy and to walk humbly with your God' (Mic 6:8 NIV).

Whose property?

Allegiance involves security. Today the Western world knows only too well the pressure of materialism: it comes at us from advertising, TV and business. We are pressurized to find our security in material wealth at the expense of the spiritual dimensions and responsibilities of our lives. It is a tension not peculiar only to modern times. Jesus saw this issue of security as one which would eventually determine our true allegiance: 'You cannot serve both God and money.' Whose property are we? To whom do we belong? Where is our true allegiance? Luke points out that when Jesus said this, the Pharisees—who were lovers of money—scoffed at him. There is little denying that for most people in the affluent West, material wealth, as a goal for personal security, exerts a powerful hold on our imaginations and hearts. Yet we cannot escape the radical alternative—privilege means responsibilities. Jesus' response was to show the Pharisees the crucial nature of kingdom responsibilities by relating a parable about an anonymous rich man and a poor man named Lazarus. This is a parable where the relationship between allegiance and security and the exercise of responsibility is made plain for all those who have ears to hear.

The parable of the rich man and Lazarus

> There was a rich man, who was clothed in purple and fine linen and who feasted sumptuously every day. And at his gate lay a poor man named Lazarus, full of sores, who desired to be fed with what fell from the rich man's table; moreover the dogs came and licked his sores.
>
> (Lk 16:19-21)

Two characters

The two protagonists in Jesus' parable are a rich man and a poor man. Each one is described in turn, so we will take them in the order they appear in the story.

The rich man first. We are told four main details about him. Three directly, and one later, by implication. The direct information concerns his financial standing, his taste for fashion and his gourmet-like enthusiasm for elaborate food. He was rich. He dressed himself in purple and fine linen. He feasted sumptuously every day.

We can imagine the kind of person. Perhaps the rich man—in the parable he is not given a particular name—owns substantial amounts of property in Beverly Hills or the West End of London. He buys his shirts from Jermyn Street or Fifth Avenue, his ties from Harrods or Bloomingdales and his tailor visits personally from Savile Row. He is a gourmet too. When he flies in by private jet to London, he takes breakfast at the Savoy Grill, has lunch at Simpsons in the Strand, tea at Claridges and dinner at the Dorchester.

The second character is a poor man named Lazarus. He is described as lying outside the gate of the rich man's house. He is very sick, covered in sores. All he can do is lie there, hoping only for some scraps thrown out with the garbage, whatever should fall 'from the rich man's table'. It is a terrible plight. He is undernourished, weak and sick. The poor man is powerless to help himself. His human dignity is utterly degraded. Even the stray dogs come and slobber all over him and lick his sores. He has not got the strength to stop them. That is the extent of his decline and misery.

Paved with gold?

Any big Western city today has sad pictures of shattered humanity just the same as the pitiful picture of Lazarus —to say nothing of the immense suffering on the streets of Calcutta and other Third World cities like her. Dick Whittington was disappointed when he found the streets of London were not paved with gold after all. Far from it! The scenes of suffering even in the affluent cities of our great Western democracies are only too obvious if we do not avert our gaze quickly enough.

When we, as a family, first moved to the West End of London to live next door to the Post Office Tower, a few moments' walk from Oxford Street and Regent Street— two of the greatest shopping areas in the world—it came as a complete eye-opener for me.

I walked up Regent Street about midnight one bitterly cold January evening. At that point I had not realized what poverty there is in London, although I had been told. In one shop there was such an ugly contrast. It was a lovely brightly lit shoe shop, selling shoes at a starting price of about one hundred and fifty pounds a pair! In the doorway of that shop, by stark contrast, there were three old men; they were unshaven, wearing torn clothes and sleeping, or trying to sleep, in cardboard boxes. I felt sick. I felt ashamed that I could think of nothing practical that I could do to help them. There are people like Lazarus just round the corner from all of us.

Two characters, the rich man and Lazarus. The one has all he wants. The other has nothing. What was that fourth detail about the rich man? It is implied when Jesus says Lazarus lay outside the gate. The word used for gate means a portico—like the entrance to a palace or a city. The rich man's house was huge, and Lazarus was obviously placed by the main entrance. The rich man could not have missed him. But from what is implied, he clearly did nothing. As Lazarus lay there day after day after day, no action was taken.

That scene provides a clue to the meaning of this parable. It is not a condemnation of wealth or riches as such. There is not so much wrong with material wealth, it is how we use wealth which is the real question. It is an issue of kingdom responsibilities, about which we will need to comment further later on. For the while, Jesus places before us the two characters, a rich man and a poor man.

Two destinations

'The poor man died and was carried by the angels to Abraham's bosom. The rich man also died and was buried; and in Hades, being in torment, he lifted up his eyes, and saw Abraham far off and Lazarus in his bosom' (Lk 16:22-23).

We are all going somewhere. Our lives all have a destination or destinations. We have to come to terms with our own mortality and realize our lives do have a destination beyond death. Jesus' teaching on this subject is unanimous in its approach. The right question to ask is not, Is there life after death? But, What kind of life is there after death?

So, what are the options? Jesus' unambiguous answer in this parable is that there are two kinds of life after death—heaven and hell. The decision and actions of the present, and our personal response to Jesus, determine which destination we will arrive at in the future. What characterizes our lives deep down? What is our true security? Where is our true allegiance? That determines our future in God's hands. There are two possible destinations.

Destination one. 'The poor man died and was carried by the angels to Abraham's bosom.'

He died. But for this poor man, his death marks a reversal in fortunes. The angels carry him to Abraham's bosom. The language here, about angels and the patriarch's bosom, may sound unfamiliar to us. But it is not too obscure upon investigation. The angels speak of the caring activity of God. The Lord lovingly brings this poor man to the place of rest, refreshment and joy in heaven. It is a typical Jewish way of speaking about heaven. The metaphor about Abraham's bosom may indicate close fellowship with Abraham (cf. Jn 13:23) at the messianic banquet.

Obviously the poor man's fortunes were reversed. But as the story progresses it becomes clear that the rich man was taken to a place where he truly belonged.

Destination two. 'The rich man also died and was buried; and in Hades, being in torment, he lifted up his eyes, and saw Abraham far off and Lazarus in his bosom' (Lk 16:22-23).

He went from riches to rags. It was a place of torment. The rich man was separated from God. Hades means the place of the dead. And it is clearly implied, as the parable develops, that this is a permanent separation of the rich man from God. It is a tragedy of the rich man's own making. There clearly are, in the forceful reality to which this parable refers, two destinations.

How can a loving God send anyone to hell? It is an important question, because it sounds like a contradiction in terms.

A loving God does not actually send anyone to hell. If anyone ends up in hell it has everything to do with their own decision. The biblical understanding of hell is one of eternal separation from the presence and person of God, and it is, therefore, a place of absolute torment.

If we shut God out of our lives now, making the decision that we do not want anything to do with him and his ways; if we refuse the offer from Jesus of a brand new life to know and serve God as the real basis of what we are meant to be as human beings; if we say no to God now—why should anything change when we die?

Domesday. Nine hundred years ago, William the Conqueror, King of England and Duke of Normandy, sent out commissioners to survey the country he had taken by force some twenty years before. Information about the people of England and their landholdings was collected and collated in volumes amounting to some two million words. It was a record of immense value and authority throughout the period of the middle ages. Within ninety years of its compilation it had acquired the nickname 'Domesday'. The record was fixed. It was a true and faithful picture of the facts; and like the book of life itself, from which its popular name was derived, there was no appeal against it.

There will be a day of judgement, a day when the full reality of our lives will be completely revealed and thoroughly cross-examined—to see precisely where we have stood in relationship to God and the responsibilities of his kingdom: 'And I saw the dead, great and small, standing before [God], and books were opened. Also another book was opened, which is the book of life. And the dead were judged by what was written in the books, by what they had done' (Rev 20:12).

If God is shut out now, he will be shut out then. God simply underwrites and underlines our decision. He cannot take the decision for us, though he does long that we should not ruin ourselves. This is why he sent Jesus to die as a substitute, to enable the kingdom of God to become a living reality. The measure of God's concern for us is Jesus' sacrifice on the cross to offer us the possibility of heaven. And it is one of the prime reasons Jesus himself tells this parable.

Jesus offers forgiveness and a new start to those who are prepared to follow him and his teaching. But we all have to beware of complacency. Complacency about spiritual matters is in the end foolhardy. Here we have an example to warn us. Complacency badly rebounded on the rich man.

Two conversations

There are two conversations, or rather two parts to the conversation. The first part of the conversation is between the rich man and Abraham. As the rich man speaks, he reveals his unchanged character: 'He called out, "Father Abraham, have mercy upon me, and send Lazarus to dip the end of his finger in water and cool my tongue; for I am in anguish in this flame"' (Lk 16:24).

The unchanged character of the rich man is obscenely obvious: 'Send Lazarus. You tell Lazarus to get up off his backside and do something useful for a change. I am parched to death down here. You remember, Lazarus used to sun himself all day in front of my house. My house! You tell him he's got a debt or two to repay me. You send him along. Send Lazarus.'

The rich man reveals his unchanged character. As Abraham replies, he reveals God's unchanged decision:

> Son, remember that you in your lifetime received your good things, and Lazarus in like manner evil things; but now he is comforted here, and you are in anguish. And besides all this, between us and you a great chasm has been fixed, in order that those who would pass from here to you may not be able, and none may cross from there to us.

(Lk 16:25-26)

God's decision is unchanged. The rich man squandered his opportunities. In his lifetime he received good things. But there is not a shred of evidence of anything but self-centredness in his character. The opportunity to help someone was laid at his very gate. He did not lift a finger to help.

The rich man's character has not changed. That is why God's decision is unchanged. Unless we take seriously the radical call to repentance, we remain locked into selfishness. We are not necessarily as selfish as this rich man—this is an extreme example to make the point but all the same, we are selfish enough to insist on our own way, keeping God and his claims at a distance, and rejecting God's final say in our affairs.

If we are like that, we will hate heaven. Heaven is a place where God comes first, others second, and self comes last. It would be the very reversal of all we stood for. It would be like asking a teetotaller to spend the rest of his life in a brewery. It would be a totally foreign environment for us. 'If we are going to live in heaven, we have to be naturalized or else we die,' so said the novelist Charles Williams, with remarkable spiritual insight.

Jesus is saying that in the life beyond there is a great chasm fixed between those who receive Jesus' gift of new life through repentance and faith, and those who insist on going their own way. There will be a chasm. There is no going back. The time of opportunity is now. Fortunes will be reversed. For some it will be from riches to rags. It is topsy-turvy teaching. It turns the accepted values of life on their head. The parable has a chilling end which carries a clear warning: some people can put off their decision in these things one day too many.

The rich man's character and decision remained unchanged. The second conversation revolves round the rich man's appeal for an easier way, an assured future. The rich man asks that Lazarus should be sent along to warn his family, his five brothers, of the miseries in store if they do not mend their ways . . . 'Come on Abraham. Can't you make it easier for them? Get old Lazarus to get out there and tell them.' To which Abraham replies, 'They have Moses and the prophets; let them hear them.' They have the Bible's message. God has sent prophets from Moses onwards. He has sent his Son Jesus Christ. These are the ones they should listen to. They have the complete message of God. There is nothing for Lazarus to add. 'Now look here Abraham, if someone were to rise from the dead, surely then they will get their lives sorted out.'

Here comes the irony. If they do not hear Moses and the prophets, neither will they be convinced if someone should rise from the dead. If they are not prepared to take account of the Bible's message, then they are hardly going to be impressed by the resurrection, are they?

'You make it so hard Abraham.'

'What's hard is your heart.'

Which is hard? The way of God or the heart of man? The parable of the rich man and Lazarus reveals two characters with two very different destinations. Their fortunes are reversed, as these two conversations show. The implication of this story is not that we can earn our way into heaven by our good deeds. It is far from saying that. The rich man was clearly nothing more than a nominal believer. He refers to Abraham as Father, showing his Jewish background. But that is all there is. There is nothing in his life to show either that he has listened responsively to the Bible's message of new life for those who humble themselves before God or that he has taken into account the prophets' teaching about the manner of life appropriate to the people of God.

Who is the rich man today? Undoubtedly, in our affluent society, the rich man is you and he is me. For all of us are rich in a variety of ways. Rich in opportunity, education, ability, and rich financially. This is certainly so when judged by the standards of some people on the edge of life in our cities and towns, and most definitely by comparison with the poor nations of the world.

This parable of Jesus is not a condemnation of wealth as such. But it does raise, among other things, the question of what we should do with our wealth. And it revolves around what is the basis of our personal security.

Four questions

The message of God. Have you taken, and are you taking, practical account of God's message? James' letter tells us to be 'doers of the word, and not hearers only' (Jas 1:22). We can deceive ourselves into thinking we are acting in a perfectly acceptable fashion, while all along ignoring what God is saying through his word. Is God still waiting for us to respond to his message?

Kingdom responsibilities are radical. God has spoken clearly and unequivocally through the prophets about his abhorrence of injustice, poverty and the structural sin which so often gives rise to it. As the eighth-century prophet Amos makes clear, we all have responsibilities that extend beyond the borders of our homes, societies and nations, to act where there is injustice of any kind— and to act with the passion of God.

Responsibility to God. Are you taking the opportunities to exercise responsibility socially, to God's glory? Moses and the prophets are full of God's concern for the poor, the sick, the underprivileged. Is there something on your own doorstep that you can do to help someone in need, perhaps by visiting the elderly or the sick, or by doing something concrete in the way of practical help? The exercise of social responsibility is, according to this parable, to the glory of God. To neglect this is to betray the kingdom.

Money. Are you spending your money in the interests of God? Are you giving to his work? We are all rich, relatively speaking. We all have enough to be able to give something. The biblical norm for Christian giving is about 10% of our pre-tax income. That is the tithe. But there is no fixed rule about it. It is more a matter of giving generously and out of the abundance God has given us, remembering and believing that God supplies all our needs.

Giving helps our deep down security to get properly anchored, and it serves the interests of God. Which is more radical, revolution or repentance? To change the economic system by force, or to redirect the wealth of nations by a revolution of love, concern and action towards the poor? Surely the latter is the truly radical alternative.

Talents. Are you using your talents, your gifts, in the service of God? We are all rich in various abilities. And, as we have already learnt, God means each one of us to have some form of ministry. Do you view your life as given in the service of Christ? Kingdom people have kingdom concerns to respond to. We are the body of Christ. He has no other arms but our arms, and no other hands than ours.

Opportunity knocks

These are important, indeed vital issues for us today. But all these questions were the clear opportunities of at least one privileged character in Jesus' parable of the rich man and Lazarus. There were two characters, two destinations and two conversations. It seems from those conversations that the rich man had every opportunity to take account of God's message and to exercise his social responsibility for God's glory. He could have spent his money in the interests of God and used his talents in the service of God. Instead, the rich man put off that opportunity. But opportunity will not last for ever. There came a moment for the rich man when opportunity came to an end, and it was all too late.

Living for the kingdom

The message is unambiguous. We must not shirk our opportunities. There comes a point in the life of every dedicated follower of Jesus when the pressures of existence, the temptations to compromise, and the whole question of how to live rightly for God become an issue requiring definite guidelines for kingdom life. Jesus not only made clear the basic issue of security, and therefore of allegiance to God, he also was at pains to point out the true basis for the exercise of kingdom responsibilities, and how those responsibilities can be effectively discharged.

Right living depends on a right relationship

'If you love me, you will keep my commandments' (Jn 14:15).

Jesus reiterates that remark in different ways twice more in John 14: 'He who has my commandments and keeps them, he it is who loves me' (v.21) and 'If a man loves me, he will keep my word' (v.23).

Right living depends on a right relationship. The relationship is to Jesus himself, and it is characterized, above all, by love.

Every father or mother knows that they do not respond to children out of duty. It is because they love them that they are prepared to respond to their children with tremendous devotion and even sacrifice. It is because of love that they want to please them and be involved in their concerns and interests, sharing together in life with them.

This is the point Jesus is making. If we love him we will respond to him, share our lives with him, take regular account of his interests and concerns for us. In short, we will keep his commandments.

What does loving Jesus mean? The first stage is to simply admire Jesus. It is more of a reaction than anything else. When you read and understand Jesus' teaching in the gospels, see him as a man and perceive what he stands for, then your reaction is one of growing admiration and esteem. When you take the further step of recognizing that Jesus, when he died, died for you— that he went through physical and spiritual agony for you—then committing your life to him, you become more and more grateful for what he has done for you and for what he means to you as the weeks, months and years go by. Admiration and gratitude grow eventually into love for Jesus.

Jesus' own highest concern is for the way we live as his followers. If we have not entered into this relationship with Jesus, we will not be concerned to respond in love to him by the commitment of our lives, and his strength and power will be denied us. This is the first direction. Right living depends on a right relationship with Jesus.

A right relationship implies obedience of lifestyle

'If you love me, you will keep my commandments' (Jn 14:15).

Jesus is saying, 'If you genuinely admire me, if you are genuinely grateful to me, if you in fact *love* me, then why do you not do what I want you to do?'

Obedience is an unpopular word these days. It has

perhaps something to do with uncaring authority, or if not uncaring, then ill-informed authority. I heard of a piano teacher who, every time her pupil played a wrong note, took a ruler and rapped the pupil over the knuckles—poor educational practice, but not unknown.

None of us likes the kind of authority which raps us over the knuckles in any sphere of life. And we do not care too much to be obedient to that kind of authority. Yet Jesus is different. His is the ultimate authority in the universe. But he rules by love, by deep understanding of our needs.

The fact is, we still rebel against his authority. Why is that? The Bible's answer is that, being fallen creatures, we would rather please ourselves. We would rather follow our natural inclinations than please anyone else, including God. Unless, that is, two things happen: a) Jesus himself comes into our life, and b) conversion is matched by our willingness to follow and obey him.

Here are two contrasting illustrations. The first concerns a girl who asked to come to see a Christian counsellor. She wanted to discuss some disturbing feelings of guilt from which she was suffering. She was a pleasant intelligent Christian girl. She had been to university, she had a responsible job. After some discussion of the background to these unsettling guilt feelings which she complained of, it emerged she was sleeping regularly with her boyfriend. The counsellor tried to point out to her, as gently and caringly as he could, that there might be a connection between the two; between behaviour which she knew as a Christian was inappropriate—that is sleeping with her boyfriend—and her guilt feelings. She agreed. Yet all she wanted was that the guilt *feelings* should be taken away. She was not prepared to change her behaviour. In the end she admitted she simply wanted to please herself. Obviously there was little else the counsellor could do for her.

The second illustration involves another person, a different situation and an altogether different outcome. This person was very distressed about the tensions in his marriage. He was always exploding with anger against his wife and children. In the end he was very much helped by Jesus' words: 'If you love me, you will keep my commandments.'

This man really *worked* on his anger. He was prepared to change. He disciplined himself in the things he said, and the way he said them. He said several times he wanted to obey Jesus' commandments, and put them into practice. It was a terrific help to him to discover that obedience is, in experience, the way to liberty. Today his marriage is restored and the family are going from strength to strength as Christians.

Learning obedience

We have to learn to obey. It is helpful for us to realize that there is something within us impeding our progress, asserting all too often our own self-will and independence. But the way of liberty is to take seriously and obey the teaching of Jesus. It does not come easily, but it is necessary. Obedience is the way to liberty.

That is why it is so important to be exposed day by day to the teaching of Scripture. Do you read and take to heart part of the Bible every day? You cannot keep Jesus' commandments if you do not know them. You make yourself unnecessarily weak for the Christian life if you neglect Scripture. It is a provision of God for us. A right relationship implies obedience of lifestyle.

Obedience releases the power of God—through the Holy Spirit

It is not surprising to learn that verse 16 of John 14 follows verse 15! But that order of events is highly significant. Taken together those two verses introduce a strengthening perspective, for God's power comes to us in the context of our obedience: 'If you love me, you will keep my commandments. And I will pray the Father, and he will give you another Counsellor, to be with you for ever.'

If you have ever felt a sense of failure and of powerlessness, having often asked God for power to change, yet finding yourself back at square one with your same old failure—and being seemingly impotent to do anything about it—then here is help from Jesus for you.

God's power comes to us in the context of our obedience. After saying that if we love him, we will obey his commandments, Jesus immediately promises the help of the Holy Spirit. Do you notice the order of events? When we obey, *then* we will know his power. Not the other way round. That order is crucial. Some people pray: 'Lord, I am so weak in this particular area. Please give me power, Lord, and strengthen me to overcome.' It is a perfectly legitimate prayer. But Jesus says, 'Be obedient, and then I'll give you strength and power.' We have to co-operate. So our prayer can now be, 'Lord, I promise that today I'm going to do something about this. So please strengthen me with your Spirit as I co-operate with you by my obedience.' It is not the form of words that matters, it is the understanding of God's priorities. This makes all the difference. God's power comes to us in the context of our obedience to him.

Four descriptions of the Spirit

In John 14, in the context of dedicated living, Jesus gives the Holy Spirit four different descriptions.

In verse 16 the Spirit is described as the Counsellor. The Greek word *Parakleton* is even better translated as a companion, one who comes alongside us. He is to us as a friend.

In verse 17 he is the Spirit of truth. The Holy Spirit is concerned for truth. So the Spirit will help us at the point where we desire to put God's truth into action.

In verse 18 Jesus says: 'I will come to you.' In the context, Jesus is not referring here to his second coming but is saying that the Spirit who is to come will be the Spirit of none other than Jesus himself.

And in verse 23, to be even more explicit, Jesus says, 'We will come to you.' That is the Father and Jesus. The Holy Spirit is in very reality the Spirit of God.

Put that teaching together, and what do we have?

The Holy Spirit is alongside us as our companion and friend. Where we go, therefore, *he* goes. In our joys, he is there; in our sorrows, he is there. He is there alongside us in our work. He is there as we search for a new job. He is there when temptation strikes, or when human strength fails. In the deepest sense, he is our companion. He is there to help us face the challenges life brings. He is there in the hospital ward. He is there when we die. He is the companion.

The Holy Spirit is the Spirit of truth. This means he is able uniquely to guide us in the ways of God, which for most of us, at least sometimes, can involve a real struggle. He knows the manufacturer's instructions inside out and backwards. He wrote them. There is no one better to keep us up and running. He is the Spirit of truth.

The Holy Spirit is the Spirit of Jesus. When Jesus says: 'I will come to you,' it means that, because he is the Spirit of Jesus, the Holy Spirit understands our weakness and sensitivity and frailty. Jesus shared our human experience for thirty-three years. He understands the struggles, both yours and mine. We are talking about a God who has total inside working knowledge of the conditions we work under as human beings.

The Holy Spirit is the Spirit of power. Jesus seems to emphasize this in verse 23, when he says the Father and Jesus will come to the one who loves and obeys Jesus and his word.

What kind of power has the Father demonstrated? The Father made all things. He is the Creator. What kind of power has Jesus demonstrated? Jesus has redeemed all things. He has conquered even death itself. That is what we mean when we speak of 'almighty' God. The Father and Jesus will come in the power of the Spirit to the one who obeys Jesus' teaching. There is and can be no greater power available to us in the whole universe.

We need to be clear on Jesus' third direction. Obedience releases the power of God through the Holy Spirit. It is a pledge—of strength and power and help—to those who take seriously his priorities. Our kingdom responsibilities involve obedience to Jesus in every realm of life.

Have you ever felt unable to find strength to overcome the issues before you? For all of us there is the daily challenge of living our lives in a way that is both honouring to and committed to Jesus Christ. It involves our thoughts, aspirations and goals; what we say and how we say it; our actions and our activities; the way we use our money and our giving—in fact our whole Christian service.

What does Jesus say to us today on this matter?

Right living depends on a right relationship to Jesus. A right relationship implies obedience in our lifestyle. And obedience itself releases the power of God through the Holy Spirit. There are three directions: love, obedience and power. That is the order of events. If, from love for Jesus Christ, we respond with obedience in the issues which really challenge our overcomfortable Western lives—even though that may be a struggle for us—God himself will respond with all the power and strengthening of his mighty Holy Spirit.

We all have kingdom responsibilities. We have to seek carefully to respond where God is placing his emphasis and concerns before us: 'He has showed you, O man, what is good. And what does the Lord require of you? To act justly and to love mercy and to walk humbly with your God' (Mic 6:8). Where is God challenging you about your lifestyle?

A kingdom without a king?

The kingdom of God is only authentically present where God's people are present. Since the kingdom is a community concept, both King and subjects have to be in evidence to authenticate its reality. If Christ the King is not present through his people, it is no use imagining that every act of mercy or kindness is a kingdom act. A kingdom without a king runs entirely counter to the biblical witness. This is to take the attributes of human-

ness that are present in all men by virtue of their creation in the image of God, and to confuse them with
Christ's redemptive work and concerns in bringing in
the new order of the kingdom of God. But if humanists
and secularist exercise, as they often do, a deeply caring
compassion for those on the edges of our communities
and society, how much more should followers of Christ
be concerned for the responsibilities of the kingdom,
and the passionate concerns of the King himself?

For all of us, what is required is a deep repentance
from the self-satisfied ways of a largely middle-class
culture, for that culture spells anything but freedom for
very large numbers of people who, for reasons beyond
their power to control, are alienated in our society and
our world.

Repentance within, not revolution without, is the
message of Jesus for those who would take kingdom
responsibilities to themselves with a new and radical
seriousness. It is the attitudes which must change if the
wrongs are to be put right. Privilege equals responsibility in a world where God desires his reign to spread
with healing grace to all mankind. There will come a day
when the opportunity to help will come to an end. But,
for the present, there remains only one question over
which Jesus the King requires our response: Are we
going to be obedient?

10

Kingdom Expectations

The powers of the new age

In John 16 Jesus speaks more comprehensively about the work of the Holy Spirit than in any other single passage in all four gospels. As we follow Jesus today, this passage is important in enabling us to gain right perspectives on kingdom reality and to form right expectations of the powers of the new age. We find ourselves in a world that is often hostile to the claims of Christ, and in which many struggles and issues need to be faced. Rightly formulated kingdom expectations are essential for those who are committed to overcoming the dangers and discouragements of a world system that fundamentally opposes the rule of God.

Opposition and discouragement

All of us face struggles. In our personal lives, sadly, we will often know broken relationships, illness, unemployment and other painful facts of living. Christians are not immune from any of these. Yet followers of Christ will often face additional pressures; opposition because of concern for kingdom values; discouragement when seeking to follow Jesus whole-heartedly in a particular situation; even scorn, when wanting to be an effective witness to family, friends, or colleagues.

We have to live with opposition and discouragement. The question is: How are we to face it? How can we cope with it day by day? What should be our expectations of the kingdom, and its power to overcome? This discouraging situation is what Jesus anticipates when he speaks to the disciples in John 16 about the Holy Spirit. The underlying truth is this: God will always be bigger and more powerful than any human situation of opposition and discouragement, however bitter or vast that problem may seem to be.

Preventing breakdown

There is a clear concern in Jesus' mind concerning the disciples' response to opposition and discouragement: 'I have said all this to you to keep you from falling away' (Jn 16:1).

Jesus has been speaking to the disciples, from John 15:18 onwards, of the inevitability of persecution; they will have to face persecution in the immediate days ahead. When Jesus said these words, he had just begun to speak to them of the promise of the Holy Spirit. He describes him as the Counsellor, the Spirit of truth, in John 15:26. Jesus' words in John 16:1 are built on all this. The coming of persecution and the coming of the Spirit are spoken of in the same breath. They are the pivot of the whole passage, and we have to keep the two together.

The New English Bible gives the best translation of John 16:1. It puts Jesus' words in this remarkably striking way: 'I have told you all this to guard you against the breakdown of your faith.' According to Jesus, this is the way to prevent spiritual breakdown, to guard against folding-up spiritually. None of us is immune. All of us are vulnerable. But Jesus' teaching is very realistic and contains two elements that are to be held together. They form the overall balance and emphasis in Jesus' kingdom expectations for living in the present world order.

First, persecution, opposition and discouragement are all real. In some shape or form, they will come to each of us. We must expect them, face them, and not run away from them. That is spiritual realism.

Second, God the Holy Spirit is more powerful than any human or even devilish opposition. His work continues triumphant even when from our human perspective the outlook perhaps look bleak. The Counsellor, the Holy Spirit, is not lacking in wisdom or power. That equally is spiritual realism.

Four dynamics of the Spirit

The promise of the Counsellor

> I did not say these things to you from the beginning, because I was with you. But now I am going to him who sent me; yet none of you asks me, 'Where are you going?' But because I have said these things to you, sorrow has filled your hearts. Nevertheless I tell you the truth: it is to your advantage that I go away, for if I do not go away, the Counsellor will not come to you; but if I go, I will send him to you.
>
> (Jn 16:4-7)

Jesus specifically says that he is mentioning these facts because he is returning to the Father. This means two things. Jesus is going to be forcibly arrested and put to death. The obvious consequence is that the disciples will be left to manage on their own—without the personal help and encouragement of Jesus. From his words, the disciples are obviously overwhelmed with sorrow at the thought of all this. They love Jesus—they do not want him to go. Because it is a hostile world, and because they are human, they may well be terrified as to how they will manage without him.

In the light of this, Jesus' comment is extraordinary. 'I tell you the truth: it is to your advantage that I go away.' In what possible sense? What is he getting at? How can Jesus' parting be advantageous?

By dying on the cross and taking on to himself the penalty of the sin in our lives, Jesus is able to bring us to life spiritually. When we come into that relationship with him, the Holy Spirit comes immediately into our personalities. He strengthens and guides us. He starts working from inside, us, rebuilding us as kingdom people who are committed to God's service.

Unless we have received Jesus' forgiveness and turned away from wrong ways, the Holy Spirit will not be able to come to us; he is unable to come because, deep down, we are still antagonistic to God. That is the state of any person not committed to Christ, however likeable. That is why Jesus has to go away; he has to die to make it possible to deal decisively with our basic antagonism to God.

Winning friends and influencing people. During his human life Jesus was able to influence probably only a few hundred people at the most, certainly not many thousands. In the end only a handful of committed disciples remained. But it was ultimately to their advantage that he went away. The coming of the Holy Spirit not only transformed their lives but as a consequence of their testimony Jesus has found his way into the hearts of millions and millions of lives all the way down the centuries. His cross is the way of forgiveness and his Spirit is the way of strength and power for living for him in this world; it enables us to face any hurdle or issue which confronts our lives.

'It is to your advantage that I go away, for if I do not go away, the Counsellor will not come to you; but if I go, I will send him to you.'

The Greek word translated, *Parakleton*, means a friend or companion, one who comes alongside us. What is the word-picture Jesus is using there? It is a simple one. Where we go, he goes—right into the situation where it is tough, where there is opposition, where there is discouragement. 'I will send him to you.'

The ministry of the Counsellor

'And when he comes, he will convince the world concerning sin and righteousness and judgment: concerning sin, because they do not believe in me; concerning righteousness, because I go to the Father, and you will see me no more; concerning judgment, because the ruler of this world is judged' (Jn 16:8-11).

The first aspect of the Holy Spirit's ministry, according to Jesus, is to convict of sin. The word translated convict, is the Greek word *elegchein*. It is the word used in the ancient Greek-speaking world to describe cross-examination in a law court, when someone is on trial. When someone who is guilty is cross-examined, one of two things can happen. If that person puts in a plea of not guilty, either the cross-examination can convict him outright of the wrong things he has done, or it can convince him of the weight of the evidence against him and the weakness of his own case, the result being a change of plea from not guilty to guilty. *Elegchein* has this double meaning of convict as well as convince.

The power of conviction. Billy McIlwaine is from Northern Ireland. He has a wonderful wife and daughter both of whom suffered terribly over the years, but they prayed constantly for him and eventually the Holy Spirit convinced and convicted him of his sins. Stated boldly, like this, Billy's story may seem unremarkable, until you realize that for many years he was a member of an illegal paramilitary organization. He was a terrorist, with a reputation for being both vicious and aggressive. To say that he hated the Catholics in Northern Ireland is a considerable understatement. When he started off in terrorism, on his own admission, the only good Catholics were dead Catholics, as far as he was concerned.

Some years ago Billy started to drink very heavily. Eight years ago, with his marriage practically in ruins, and wanted by the police, he was regularly consuming three bottles of whisky a day. In a Channel 4 interview on British television, he described how, back in 1979, he lay in a hospital bed, his cirrhosis of the liver so advanced that the consultant told his family he would be lucky to live for even a few weeks. Billy McIlwaine said that lying there, facing death, something happened which was one of those rare moments in a person's life

—a moment where your whole life flashes before you. And he said how, at that moment, he realized for the first time ever, how awful, how bad, how disgusting his life had been. For the first time, this bitter, hardened terrorist was actually convinced about his sin.

Dying in his hospital bed in Northern Ireland, Billy cried to God for forgiveness. And he prayed: 'Lord, if there is room in your heart to forgive someone as foul as I am, then I'll dedicate whatever life I have left to serving you, by loving those I have only sought to hate, despise and destroy' [reproduced by permission of A + 4].

In fact he lived and today he is a changed man. Now with a Christian group called Soldiers of the Cross, Billy works for reconciliation between Protestants and Catholics in Northern Ireland; this involves helping paramilitaries who have been either violent or murderers to leave terrorism and come to Christ. It is very dangerous work. He himself is on a hit list. But the transformation of his life is clear for all to see: now his marriage is wonderfully restored, his health is saved, and he is a strong and loving Christian. He actually loves the people he once hated. How clearly all this is a result of the Holy Spirit.

Conviction is the first step for which to pray. When we are concerned for another person to become a Christian, we should pray that the Spirit will convince them of their need and convict them of their sin. It is God, and God alone, who breaks down the barriers of indifference, resistance and sin itself. This is the first role of the Holy Spirit. We have to remember this, otherwise we can become deeply unsettled. Salvation, from the beginning to the end, depends on God. We do have our part to play; but it rests ultimately on the Spirit's transcendent power, not on our unreliable human contributions. The first work of the Spirit is to convict of sin. Sometimes, as in the case of Billy McIlwaine, the work of conviction will take many, many years to come to fruition. But the Lord knows what he is doing. He never leaves anything to chance. He can get through to anyone.

The revelation of the Counsellor

'I have yet many things to say to you, but you cannot bear them now. When the Spirit of truth comes, he will guide you into all the truth' (Jn 16:12-13).

The reason Jesus sends the Spirit into our tangled human experience is to straighten us out so that we can live full, enriched lives which are truly honouring to God. We have seen that already. So hand in hand with Jesus' power, which is deep at work in our hearts, is Jesus' word—his truth—at work in our minds.

To change a person's behaviour you have to influence both his mind and his will. In order to be fully equipped with the powers of the new age, we need God's word as much as his Spirit. Here in Jesus' teaching we see that the two go together. That is why Jesus says to the disciples that although he still has many things to say to them, the Holy Spirit himself will take over that role and guide them to perceive all the truth Jesus wants to make known to them, and to us.

What does this mean as far as the Bible is concerned? In one sense this is Jesus' promise for the inspiration of the New Testament. The disciples already had Jesus' words. We know that the gospels were compiled from collections of Jesus' sayings and reports of his actions made by the disciples. Yet here is a promise of further revelation. It is a promise geared to the writings and teachings of the apostles. The writings of the New Testament are guaranteed to tell unique truth which contains God's power to change us effectively when we allow it to positively influence our minds and lives. It was Jesus who promised and guaranteed the inspiration of the New Testament. It was a promise to the apostolic authors: 'He will guide you into all the truth.'

The focus of the Counsellor

'He will glorify me, for he will take what is mine and declare it to you' (Jn 16:14).

The Holy Spirit has a spotlight ministry. He throws the focus entirely upon Jesus. Above the entrance to

Broadcasting House, the home of the BBC in London, next door to All Souls Church, Langham Place, there is an impressive carving. It is of two figures, and depicts Prospero sending Ariel out into the world. Late at night a spotlight from the other side of the road, high up in the Langham Hotel, is focused specifically on to those two figures. It makes them stand out vividly. It is a shaft of light, cutting clear across Langham Place, causing attention to go straight to that carving of Prospero and Ariel. They are spotlighted for everyone to see. There is no missing them.

The Holy Spirit has a spotlight ministry. He focuses entirely on Jesus. He is the one who prompts us to glorify Jesus in what we say and think and do. He makes Jesus stand out in our understanding, our desire to serve him, and the way Jesus is perceived by others. He throws all the attention on to Jesus. So to glorify Jesus should equally be our goal. We should want to throw the spotlight on to him.

If we respond to the conviction that the Holy Spirit brings when we are in the wrong, if we obey the teaching that he has inspired and which itself comes from Jesus, then we are in a position to serve and honour Jesus with our daily lives—to glorify him. In this way, we ourselves throw the spotlight on to Jesus.

Jesus points out four dynamics concerning the Spirit, the Counsellor: the promise, the ministry, the revelation, and the focus. Jesus said that he mentioned these four dynamics to guard against the breakdown of our faith. Faith is always going to be under pressure. The Christian life is always going to be difficult, for we cannot avoid struggles. But we have received the *promise* of the Counsellor. We are not alone. We have an incredibly powerful, strong friend and companion. No matter where we go, no matter what the turmoil, he goes too. He is there.

The *ministry* of the Counsellor goes on, unimpeded by human weakness or opposition. He is as able to convince and convict those about whom we care deeply, as much as he is able to convict an Irish terrorist or anyone, however hardened or pained or disillusioned. God is able to make himself known even in the face of human resistance. He convicts in order to bless.

The *revelation* of the Counsellor is the means by which to face opposition and discouragement. Most, if not all, of the New Testament was written against the background of persecution, unbelief and opposition. The word of God, the revelation of the Counsellor, the Spirit of truth, is Jesus' way of strengthening us for a struggle that, with his resources, we can face and overcome. The Scriptures are vital to our strength.

The *focus* of the Counsellor gives us a goal. Whatever situation we are involved in, whatever challenge there is before us, one question is enough: Is my response glorifying to Jesus Christ? All we need is to decide that *that* will be our goal, and the Spirit will give us strength for it to become reality. As always, the struggle will be over motivation. To glorify Jesus is the Spirit's entire concern—and he will make it happen. The spotlight must go on to Jesus, and away from ourselves.

There are two truths to hold together which will help to guard against the breakdown of faith. The first is a right understanding of kingdom reality. There are bound to be times of difficulty, discouragement and opposition. In a real sense, they are opportunities to face up to our commitment to the King and to grow in his grace. The second thing to appreciate is that at the same time, even during such difficulties, we are not on our own. There *are* powers for the new age. God is God. His power is mightily at work within us. We should be sure to use the resources he has made available to us. The Counsellor, the Spirit of truth, is both with us and in us. Holding on to these two truths means that in opposition and discouragement, we can face the issues and overcome.

The signs of the new age

Kingdom people are called to face up to the struggles of existence, but with a new power to overcome, a power which is itself released through obedience to Christ; for the wisdom of the King, and his plans for us, will always transcend the horizons of our human perspectives. Overcoming in the present depends to a certain extent on our view of the future. In communities where there is high unemployment, with consequent social malaise, the unlikelihood of change often brings in its wake a depressing erosion in resolve and enthusiasm. Hope is an essential human dimension. Without hope, there is no future worth aspiring towards, only a promise that the next night will be as dark as all those which have gone before. We have a deep psychological need to trace the rainbow through the rain.

The apostle Paul writes that followers of Christ were saved in hope: 'But hope that is seen is no hope at all. Who hopes for what he already has? But if we hope for what we do not yet have, we wait for it patiently' (Rom 8:24-25 NIV). That hope in which we are saved is seen vividly in the ministry of Jesus, and is most graphically presented in the signs of the kingdom.

John records seven miracles of Jesus which are signs pointing both to who Jesus is, and to the nature of the kingdom he is inaugurating. He even calls them 'signs' using the Greek word *semeia*: 'Jesus did many other miraculous signs [*semeia*] in the presence of his disciples, which are not recorded in this book. But these are written that you may believe that Jesus is the Christ, the Son of God, and that by believing you may have life in his name' (Jn 20:30-31 NIV).

The seven signs of Jesus' ministry which John records are a foretaste of the messianic kingdom. They portray the hope in which we are saved. The turning of water into wine (Jn 2), the healing of the Roman officer's son (Jn 4), the cure of the Bethesda cripple (Jn 5), the feeding of the five thousand (Jn 6), the walking on the water (Jn 6), the healing of the man born blind (Jn 9), and the raising of Lazarus (Jn 11) clearly and penetratingly illustrate both the new powers of the age to come, and the supremely moving compassion of God towards the pain and alienation of the human condition. Nowhere is this combination of power linked with compassion more clearly portrayed than in the sign which is regarded by John as the culmination of all that characterizes Jesus' Messiahship—the raising of Lazarus at Bethany.

Till death us do part

Death is a subject about which everyone, practically without exception, finds it difficult both to think about and to speak of openly. Bereavement is a deeply painful and disorientating experience; and the prospect of our own death, especially when we are face to face with its real possibility, is without doubt the supreme crisis of our lives. The death of someone dear to us releases powerful emotions within us. In these circumstances, we all feel acutely the searing pain of loss and bewilderment.

Such a reality matters to us as people perhaps far more than any other hurdle that we face in our frail human experience; it touches us at the sharp end of our lives. Does the kingdom of God have anything relevant and therefore distinctive to say in these situations? Does it make the kind of difference to cause us to face our mortality with a radically different perspective and hope?

Jesus faced up to this painful subject of death. He did not surround it with the usual conspiracy of silence. The issue comes to the fore in John's gospel in the sign or miracle often described as the raising of Lazarus. It is about a death in the family.

The relevance of the situation

'Now when Jesus came, he found that Lazarus had already been in the tomb four days. Bethany was near Jerusalem, about two miles off, and many of the Jews had come to Martha and Mary to console them concerning their brother' (Jn 11:17-19).

Stage one in the investigation of the events at Bethany is to establish the relevance of this situation in relation to our own needs today. In talking about death, we need to know whether this event speaks to our own experience. Is it relevant? Or is it light years away from our world, our anxieties, our pain, our fears? Such an event, however thoughtful or moving in its own terms, will be of no practical and spiritual use to us today if it is just a dusty piece of ancient literature.

Jesus is responding to a situation of bereavement and grief. There has been a death in the family. Lazarus, the brother of Martha and Mary, has died. Funerals in that kind of climate took place much sooner than they do in our colder climates. When Jesus arrives, the funeral has already taken place; Lazarus has been in the tomb four days.

Jewish families are, and always have been, very supportive when it comes to bereavement. The special expression used by Jews is 'to sit shivvas'. It is an intriguing expression. To sit shivvas means that the most bereaved members of the immediate family are consoled, and brought food, and looked after by a wide circle of friends and relations who come and visit and sit with the bereaved for several days after the death. Sitting shivvas actually refers to the mourning stools which are brought for the bereaved to sit on at this time, while others provided help and support in various practical ways.

This process of mourning and support is exactly what was going on at Bethany: 'Many of the Jews had come to Mary and Martha to console them concerning their brother' (Jn 11:19).

This Jewish way of helping is extremely supportive. The bereaved members of the family are not expected to say or do anything in particular. Naturally there is a fair expression of grief; but there is plenty of authentic identification and sharing in the pain of loss. The Jews have a great deal to teach the Gentile world today about grieving and family support and friendship in these difficult moments of life.

The immediate relevance of this situation in which we find Jesus is that it does speak directly to our own experience of the fragility of life now. We do not need much imagination to begin to feel the sense of disorientation, pain and loss that this bereavement has brought to the family of Lazarus.

Before Lazarus dies, when the two sisters send the message to Jesus that he is sick (Jn 11:3), the sense of uncertainty, fear and panic behind their few brief words can almost be tangibly felt. It is exactly the same kind of emotional experience that we can encounter today.

We can all identify emotionally with Martha and Mary, the bereaved sisters. But at a deeper level an identification needs to be made in a different sense, not just with the bereaved, but also with Lazarus, the person who has died. Our lives *are* very fragile. The fact is we just do not know how long we have to live.

We can easily and unwittingly be complacent about the future. We take it for granted. But there are no guarantees of any kind. There is a built-in precariousness about life which we have both to reckon with, and take seriously in our thinking. And more than that, we have to prepare for these eventualities practically and spiritually.

Jesus *is* speaking to a relevant situation. This is the sort of situation in which we might find ourselves—not just emotionally, but practically speaking too. It is an issue we all have to face. It is not just other people's death we have to cope with, most of all it is our own.

Facing the issue

The second stage in understanding the sign of Lazarus involves the way Jesus both changes and challenges our perspectives on the subject of death.

The climax of the conversation between Martha and Jesus comes when Jesus says: 'I am the resurrection and the life; he who believes in me, though he die, yet shall he live, and whoever lives and believes in me shall never die' (Jn 11:25-26). These are remarkable words; by them, Jesus changes our perspectives on death.

The perspective-changers. There are many important instances in history where individuals, by their words, actions or discoveries, have dramatically changed the way we see things. In 1530, Nicolaus Copernicus was the man who discovered that the sun was the centre of the solar system. It was revolutionary; it literally changed perspectives. In 1628, William Harvey discovered the circulation of the blood. It is hard to imagine how important that one single discovery has been in the developments in modern medicine and health care. There are so many more striking examples. Wilhelm Röntgen discovered X-rays. Isaac Newton discovered the laws of gravity. These are all people who have changed our lives. They have reorientated the way we see things.

New ways of seeing mean we change our perspectives. This is also true of the story of the raising of Lazarus. Jesus' words to Martha radically change our perspectives on the issue of human mortality, giving us a new way of seeing the whole subject of death.

What is really behind what Jesus is saying? We must be specific and find out what he is actually referring to.

Making assumptions. When we find ourselves in conversation, there are always certain things we take for granted. We make certain assumptions. There is always something behind what we say. Talk to anyone who loves the theatre: if you mention Broadway or the National to them they will know what you mean without any need for you to spell out the details—your meaning will be perfectly clear, there is no mistaking it. To the uninitiated, Rach 3 may sound like a shelf at the supermarket, but to a pianist it is unmistakable. Rach 3? Rachmaninoff's third piano concerto. Like Tchaik 1. Or even Rach Pag!

When there is a common understanding behind what we say, we normally call this a frame of reference. We do not need to spell out every single detail, because certain assumptions are common to both us and our listeners. So what was the frame of reference behind what Jesus said? What were the assumptions he made about his hearers' background knowledge?

A verse in Hebrews affords us a theological glimpse behind the scenes. It is a summary verse of much New

Testament teaching and provides the frame of reference for us on the subject of death and judgement: 'Man is destined to die once, and after that to face judgment' (Heb 9:27 NIV).

When Jesus says, 'Whoever lives and believes in me shall never die,' the whole verse is inexplicable unless something else, an unspoken but implied wider frame of reference, lies behind his words. He cannot be saying that you will never physically die if you believe in him. He never taught physical immortality—that is mythology, not Christianity. So what is he talking about? Does the verse from Hebrews 9 give us the frame of reference we need?

The implication of what Jesus is saying is about spiritual death, not physical death. It is all to do with judgement. In speaking to a godly Jewish person like Martha, the clear assumption which Jesus would make was that she would know and accept the clear Old Testament teaching that after death comes judgement. Hebrews 9:27 suggests that it was a basic part of the Jewish Christian understanding that death is followed by judgement.

Jesus' words radically alter our perspectives on death because they force us to come to terms with the fact we are accountable to God. We may fear the physical aspect of death, and most of us do. Yet there is, as Jesus clearly implies here, the possibility of eternal death—a spiritual death that is much more to be feared than physical death —and that possibility is a far, far greater issue.

When we die, and our lives are played back to us and we see ourselves as we really have been in our many weaker moments, we are going to have to agree that there is not only something wrong with us, but that we are genuinely guilty before God. After death there is the judgement; we are accountable to God.

We hardly ever consider the possibility of the spiritual dimension to death. Jesus' words force us to realize we are accountable to God. But he actually offers a way out—a final, lasting and complete solution to the problem of death. Jesus claims that he is God's unique way out. It is all tied in with his own death and resurrection. Jesus died willingly and sacrificially by Roman crucifixion. It was God's own solution to the problem of death—death understood in the widest terms; Jesus' sacrifice took both physical and spiritual death seriously. His death is a payment for sin. It means that when we stand before God at the judgement, if we have responded to Christ now, our account will be marked 'paid in full'. That is the nature and power of forgiveness. If we live and believe in him, we shall never die, because Jesus' resurrection broke death's stranglehold—he is the resurrection and the life. He enables us to face the judgement. Jesus simply holds out his love; for that love and compassion is right at the heart of the matter. It brings us to the next stage in this investigation.

Jesus' own example of pain and compassion in the face of death

'When Jesus saw [Mary] weeping, and the Jews who came with her also weeping, he was deeply moved in spirit and troubled' (Jn 11:33).

'Jesus wept' (Jn 11:35).

A profound lesson about the love of God. When someone close to us dies, part of the explanation of why we feel so desperately bereft is simply because we loved them. If there had not been any love, there would not be much sense of loss. And that is why it is right to express our grief. It is an expression of our love and therefore of the sadness we feel. In a way it is the price we pay for love.

What does this incident say to us about the love of God? The real mistake when thinking about God is to think of him in the abstract, as an idea, a concept, a force or even as distant, stern and unapproachable. God is not like that. He is personal.

At Lazarus' tomb, Jesus shows us that in a real sense God sheds tears. God loves us deeply. That picture of Jesus weeping, baring his own pain and compassion, demonstrates not only that God cares and understands, it reveals even more. God has made Jesus available to us, to help us right at the very centre of our point of need as we contemplate and face death. Real love is always

more than a feeling, it ends up with action: it always
wants to do the utmost to help and put things right.
And, of course, Jesus did not simply weep, he acted in
power and changed the situation.

Now we need to assess the actual power over death
which Jesus displays in action.

Jesus demonstrates his power

'Then Jesus, deeply moved again, came to the tomb' (Jn
11:38).

> Jesus lifted up his eyes and said, 'I thank thee that thou hast
> heard me. I knew that thou hearest me always, but I have
> said this on account of the people standing by, that they
> may believe that thou didst send me.' When he had said
> this, he cried with a loud voice, 'Lazarus, come out.' The
> dead man came out, his hands and feet bound with band-
> ages, and his face wrapped with a cloth. Jesus said to them,
> 'Unbind him, and let him go' (Jn 11:41-44).

There can be no more dramatic or moving human
event. Graveyards are bleak places. Jesus, himself
deeply upset, was surrounded by other bereaved
people. Yet what they witnessed when Jesus acted so
decisively must have been absolutely extraordinary. It is
important that we understand that more than mere
words were involved. The raising of Lazarus was an
extraordinary one-off miracle. It sprang from Jesus'
concern and compassion for Martha and Mary. But
much more than that, it was a piece of tangible evidence,
a sign that Jesus is able to do what he says he can do.

The curtain-raiser. If you go to an opera house to hear
an opera or go to a theatre to hear a musical, as the
house lights go down the orchestra or the band will always play some kind of an overture. An overture is a
kind of prelude. It gives you a taste of what is to come. It
is not the opera or show itself, but it does give you a feel
of what is on the way. It moulds your expectations. It is a
curtain-raiser. It is the sure sign that something even
better is poised to happen.

The raising of Lazarus is just such a sign. That is how
John actually describes it. He says these miracles of Jesus

are meant to be signs. They are pointers to who Jesus actually is, and they give us just a glimpse of what the coming kingdom of God will be like.

It is, in fact, a two-way sign. The raising of Lazarus points backwards to give us evidence of who Jesus really is; but it also points forward to show us what Jesus really can do. Jesus' own resurrection is the final guarantee of eternal life. The raising of Lazarus is a prelude, an overture, a curtain-raiser, a sign. It is something which points us powerfully to who Jesus is, and what he can do in the full face of death.

It is not a morbid thing to speak of death. The really morbid thing is to be *unprepared* for death.

What have these four analytical stages we have been through actually taught us? The situation as we have seen it here is a deeply relevant one to our own needs. And it is true that Jesus radically alters our perspectives on death. But Jesus' own reaction of pain and compassion speaks to us, not of a God who is distant or uncaring, but of a God who loves, who sheds tears for us, and who has, in response to our own mortality, put into action the most amazing rescue plan the world has ever seen.

The whole incident in John 11 has, then, been recorded in order to prompt us. It is true we sometimes need a jolt to prompt us, to help us see things more realistically, and to do what is necessary. On this issue only we can take responsibility for ourselves. No one else can face death for us. We have to ask ourselves whether we are facing up to that. Jesus' teaching, no matter who we are, leads us to be certain of one fact about death. One day we will all look back; then we will realize that placing our trust in Jesus was the most important choice of our whole life.

Signs and wonders today

As recorded in the gospels, Jesus' miracles are signs of God's power and compassion. They are signs of all that characterizes the hope which the kingdom embodies, and demonstrate how God's rule properly responds to the deepest longings and pains of the human heart.

> Miracles are a foreshadowing and promise of coming universal redemption and the fullness of the kingdom. Casting out demons signals God's invasion of the realm of Satan and Satan's final destruction (Matthew 12:29; Mark 3:27); Luke 11:21ff; John 12:31; Revelation 20:1ff). Healing the sick bears witness to the end of all suffering (Revelation 21:4). Miraculous provisions of food tell us about the end of all human need (Revelation 7:16ff). Stilling storms points forward to the complete victory over the powers of nature that threaten the earth. Raising the dead announces that death will be forever done away with (1 Corinthians 15:26). [John Wimber, *Power Evangelism* (Hodder & Stoughton, 1985) p.98.]

But the issue has a broad base. Are these signs of grace embedded purely in the historical reality of the *past*, speaking powerfully of future glory still yet to be revealed? Or is there, in some measure great or small, a sense in which those signs may be properly expected to be manifested today, as part of the present reality of the kingdom which Jesus has inaugurated?

Ways of seeing

Right expectations of kingdom grace today can be rightly formulated only by lining up our faith, hope and expectations for the present with an accurate picture of the biblical world-view and mandate. Do we understand God aright? Are we clear about the kind of world in which we live? What is our view of the purposes of the kingdom? What is the relation of the present to the future? What is the attitude of faith within ourselves? What does Scripture itself direct? These questions all involve various ways of seeing God, the world, the kingdom, and our own attitudes and goals. There is little point to kingdom privileges and responsibilities in the kingdom of God if it is not at all clear where God himself fits into the picture. What constitutes a right vision in such things?

The real absence

The rationalist world-view pictures God as being manifestly absent from this world. Absent either because he does not exist—the view of atheistic rationalism—or absent because, as the Creator who has made all things, he has—as an absentee landlord or watchmaker might—left the world to get on with itself, to tick away merrily for ever. This is the view of eighteenth-century deism, a form of rationalism which has been seeping into the church ever since the deists first propounded it. Both views, the non-Christian and the quasi-Christian, boil down to the same conclusion: God is absent from this world. We are on our own. In Arthur Koestler's phrase, 'God has left the receiver off the hook.' Do not expect any response from the beyond . . .

World-view determines expectations. What do we say to the assertion of the absence of God? It depends on fundamental assumptions about the world in which we live.

There are two possible ways of seeing the world. Ever since the birth of modern science through the pioneering work of Newton, Galileo, Copernicus and others, all Western thinkers have been agreed on the basic nature of the universe in which we live. There is a uniformity of natural causes in this world. When an apple falls from the tree to the ground, we expect it to happen that way next time too, and not to fall upwards! There is a uniform set of expectations built into the natural pattern of cause and effect. However, the issue for us revolves around whether the system in which these causes function is a closed or an open one. Is the world like a house with all the doors and windows locked and bolted, where no one can get in from outside? This is the position of the rationalists; however the world got there, no one is going to be allowed to tamper with it now it is here. Or is the world, like that house, a self-contained system, but one where the means of access is open, where no one has bolted anything against intruders, and God can introduce elements of change when and wherever he desires to do so?

The biblical position must be the latter, the open system; on the basis of the incarnation alone this view makes the most sense. Rationalists should also agree, on the basis of the following consideration, that it is the position of the greatest reasonableness. It is one thing to observe and agree upon the uniformity of natural causes; it is a very great leap of faith, indeed a monstrous assumption without a sufficient cause, to then assume that just because something has happened in one way before, it must, by right, happen in precisely the same way on every subsequent occasion. Of course there is an element of predictability built into our lives—otherwise we would never trust an aeroplane even to take off. But at the same time, it is going beyond the evidence to say there is no possibility of outside intervention which will change the course of events, should God decide to.

To believe in an open system is not so much *the* position of faith; in fact, the closed-system view reflects a certain kind of misconstrued faith, when it races ahead of any empirical evidence and by its arbitary exclusions demonstrates itself to be anything but scientific. The open system is quite simply an attitude of openness. It says these possibilities *may* happen; it does not rule them out from day one.

Jesus' incarnation, the incarnation of the Creator King and God as man, is a powerful pointer to the open-system view. If God was able to enter the human arena then—historically, personally, visibly and tangibly—there is no reason in principle why he should not have an involvement in the lives of individuals and the affairs of this world, and indeed the whole universe, both before and beyond that time. There is a biblical continuum from the initial statement of Genesis in Genesis 1:2 (NIV), where the Spirit of God is described as 'hovering over the waters', to the magesterial announcement of Revelation 21:3 (NIV), 'Now the dwelling of God is with men . . . .' The real presence of God in our world must mean that we are expected to be open to the working of that same Holy Spirit today.

The now and not yet of the kingdom

Jesus' miracles have an authenticating and eschato-logical dimension.

As signs they tell us about the compassion of God and his kingly sovereignty over all world affairs—the human as well as the social, the political as well as the natural. They also authenticate the Messiahship of Jesus, in that the Messiah reflects the attributes of divine kingly sove-reignty. They further illustrate the eschatological dimension, bringing forth a glimpse and foretaste of the shape of things to come. The signs point mainly beyond our time to the times as yet to be fulfilled. But in an important sense, we now live in the presence of the future, because the kingdom of God, though still un-folding, has a present reality as well as a future dimen-sion.

Jesus' claims about the arrival of the kingdom of God were unambiguous: 'If I drive out demons by the Spirit of God, then the kingdom of God has come upon you' (Mt 12:28 NIV); 'The kingdom of God is not coming with signs to be observed; nor will they say, "Lo, here it is!" or "There!" for behold, the kingdom of God is in the midst of you' (Lk 17:20-21). In one breath, Jesus clearly taught that the kingdom of God was a present reality, identi-fiable with himself. Yet he was at pains to present the unfolding kingdom as a fact both dynamically present in his own person and for the present age and also as future hope still to be revealed. The parables of the marriage feast, the tares, the talents, and the wise and foolish virgins also make this clear; as do specific sayings such as Matthew 7:21-23 and 8:11-12, which give a defi-nite future dimension to the kingdom as well.

The tension between the now and the not yet is, for us, a creative tension. On the one hand we can and should be open to the powerful working of God's Spirit to transform us inwardly, to guide our circumstances, and to bring God's gracious answers to our prayer re-quests. Nothing less can be expected: 'For the Lord is

the great God, the great King above all gods. In his hand
are the depths of the earth, and the mountain peaks
belong to him. The sea is his, for he made it, and his
hands formed the dry land' (Ps 95:3-5 NIV). At the same
time the kingdom is still unfolding. We should pray in
all circumstances (Phil 4:6); when sick, we have the right
to ask the elders of our church to pray for healing (Jas
5:13-16); there is no area of our lives, our society or our
world which we should not bathe in prayer (1 Tim 2:1-
2). All, however, must be subject to the wisdom of God,
who alone knows his best purposes for us (Rom 11:33-
36; Prov 3:5-12).

Two defective views of God distort the careful balance
the New Testament draws between the present and the
future of God. Both are sub-Christian, and both inspire
damaging extremes.

The first is a God stripped of his regal power. This is
the God with whom it is comfortable to get along. He
makes no particular demands on us. It is OK to go to
him when you are in trouble, not that it makes any
material difference, but the thought makes you feel
better. If we recoil from that idea, it is as well to reflect
that many people who are apparently committed to the
gospel of Christ hold views which effectively have the
same outcome. They do not expect God to actively unsettle their comfortable existence, at least not in ways
which would mean that he made his power and will most
actively known.

The other view, which sees God as if he were the genie
in the lamp, is the opposite extreme. Rub the lamp hard
enough and the genie appears to do your will. Some of
us tend to treat prayer like this. We tell God what he
should do; and since when we pray for healing, we are
clear that sickness does not represent the will of God, we
have no doubt that because this is what we want, it must
be what he wants anyway.

But there is always a provisionality about the New
Testament promises on prayer Jesus has made us a
conditional promise: 'You may ask me for anything in
my name, and I will do it' (Jn 14:14). This is a glorious

invitation to bring all our needs to God and submit them to the mind of Christ. Whatever is according to his supreme purposes he will do. This must be the reason for the expression 'in my name'—it means 'according to the mind of Jesus'. It is not a simple statement about the mediation of Christ. Praying in the name of Jesus means more than that. It disfigures Jesus' meaning to regard this statement as a blank cheque. We violate the nature of our relationship with God as children to the Father if, ignoring the family relationship, we do not acknowledge that our Father knows best. God can and does heal. But we should never claim healing at the expense of the wisdom of God. As our Father, we should bring all our needs to him. No prayer ever goes unanswered. It is just that we must learn to accept the answer God gives back, for this is the way of growth in discipleship. God's ultimate wisdom from his supreme vantage-point is always best for us.

Even the most committed Christians can slip into a neo-paganism when it comes to prayer; if their view of God pictures him as a glorified genie in a lamp, who is always capable of being released and summoned by impressive-sounding spells or formulae. Make no mistake, God is not bound. Nothing is beyond his power; nor is anything beyond his mind and wisdom to comprehend. Never underrate him—but never overplay your relationship to him either. Let us always have great expectations of a God who deals wisely and graciously with us according to his power revealed in the resurrection, according to the mind of Christ, and 'according to the plan of him who works out everything in conformity with the purpose of his will' (Eph 1:11 NIV).

Kingdom come

Let Paul, who was no stranger either to the painful realities of discipleship, nor the powerful workings of the Holy Spirit, have the last word about God's unfolding kingdom. A kingdom that has come and yet is still to be fully realized:

I consider that our present sufferings are not worth comparing with the glory that will be revealed in us. The creation waits in eager expectation for the sons of God to be revealed. For the creation was subjected to frustration, not by its own choice, but by the will of the one who subjected it, in hope that the creation itself will be liberated from its bondage to decay and brought into the glorious freedom of the children of God.

We know that the whole creation has been groaning as in the pains of childbirth right up to the present time. Not only so, but we ourselves, who have the firstfruits of the Spirit, groan inwardly as we wait eagerly for our adoption as sons, the redemption of our bodies. For in this hope we were saved. But hope that is seen is no hope at all. Who hopes for what he already has? But if we hope for what we do not yet have, we wait for it patiently.

In the same way, the Spirit helps us in our weakness. We do not know what we ought to pray for, but the Spirit himself intercedes for us with groans that words cannot express. And he who searches our hearts knows the mind of the Spirit, because the Spirit intercedes for the saints in accordance with God's will.

(Rom 8:18-27 NIV)

II

The Unfolding Kingdom

We live in the light of the return of the King. Jesus has promised to return to the earth as Judge of the living and the dead, and to usher in a new world order. When *he* comes, the *kingdom* comes—in complete fulfilment. Until that time, 'We must go through many hardships to enter the kingdom of God' (Acts 14:22 NIV).

Jesus' return is the pivotal event of all history; all time is converging on this one climactic moment of the King's saving dealings with this world. What will the new world order which he will bring in be like? And how should we live in the light of this pledged reality?

A new heaven and a new earth

There is a sense of finality as well as a sense of continuity in the Bible's teaching. This ordinary day-by-day human experience in which we are all involved, will one day come to an end. But what happens at the end of human history? Evolutionary optimists say our world will get better and better, 'World without end.' Tomorrow's world technologists envisage a Utopian dream of a happier, safer, cleaner world where swords will be beaten into microchips. Nuclear pessimists, on the other hand, say there is a bleak future ahead. Many are fearful that man may well destroy the planet before he has a chance to improve it. Some say: 'That will be that; when the end comes . . . that's it.' Bertrand Russell said: 'In the end—life is only triviality just for a moment. And when the end comes. Then nothing.'

Eschatology is the shorthand term used to describe the fiction, the theory and the facts about the last things of this world. But biblical eschatology is much more realistic than the evolutionary optimists' outlook, and much more challenging than the nuclear pessimists' prognostications. The Bible's teaching about the end of the world is not about coming to a full stop. It is about a new world—a world which we can confidently expect; a world that has been, in a sense, renewed; a world which involves both continuity with and discontinuity from life as we know it now. In his apocalyptic vision of the future of all things, John wrote: 'I saw a new heaven and a new earth; for the first heaven and the first earth had passed away' (Rev 21:1).

What kind of reality is envisaged?

'I thought a Christian goes to heaven when he dies, so why is there going to be a new heaven and a new earth? What's wrong with the old heaven, anyway? And why do we need a new earth if we are going to heaven?' That is what immediately comes into some people's minds when they first encounter this subject. The straightforward response is that although the Bible does not normally speak of 'going to heaven when we die', it certainly means that in its statements; but its concept of life beyond death is of a much more exciting, dynamic and stimulating environment than the simple talk of heaven conjures up in many of our minds.

The poet, Laurie Lee, justifiably criticizes a typical image or picture of heaven which he says is too chaste, too disinfected, too much on its best behaviour. In similar vein, Walter Rauschenbusch, the American social theologian, wrote in 1917:

> In the present life we are bound up with wife and children, with friends and work mates, in a warm organism of complex life. When we die, we join—what? A throng of souls, an unorganised crowd of saints, who each carry a harp, and have not even formed an orchestra.

Both Lee's and Rauschenbusch's criticisms are based on caricatures; but they are caricatures which the Christian world lamentably seems to peddle all too readily to those who look for guidance on such matters. We need to be better informed of the Bible's teaching on heaven and the new world. In the Bible, the new heaven and the new earth is at the very least a most exciting prospect. There are several reasons why the Bible speaks of a new heaven and a new earth, rather than of 'going to heaven when you die'.

In Genesis 28:12 we meet Jacob, the son of Isaac: 'And [Jacob] dreamed that there was a ladder set up on the earth, and the top of it reached to heaven; and behold, the angels of God were ascending and descending on it! This was one of those Old Testament dreams given by God as a means of revelation. What does the dream mean?

Surprisingly the dream has what we might call a New Testament fulfilment. Right at the beginning of his public ministry, Jesus says to the slightly sceptical Nathaniel, 'Truly, truly, I say to you, you will see heaven opened, and the angels of God ascending and descending upon the Son of man' (Jn 1:51). That is the first major teaching emphasis of Jesus in John's gospel. But what is Jesus referring to?

It is clear that Jesus is making a reference to Jacob's dream. So right at the start of the Bible, and right at the beginning of Jesus' ministry, this point is underlined. Heaven, which is the home or realm of God, and earth, which is the home or realm of man, are to be brought together. Heaven and earth are to be reunited. In the symbolism of Jacob's dream, it is as if a ladder or a bridge will be set up between God and man, between heaven and earth. And clearly Jesus is saying, 'I am that bridge.'

The picture of the angels coming and going is of a future but permanent interaction between God and man, between heaven and earth. While Jesus is the bridge—between divinity and humanity, between the life of heaven and life of earth—he is also the one who has inaugurated by his death, resurrection and ascension the coming of the new world. The new world is one where God and man are together. The new heaven and the new earth will not be two separate realities, they will be a *unity* between God and man. Surely this is more earthly than the caricatures of a harp-twanging heaven and yet more heavenly than the Utopian dreams of a high-technology, computer-crazed earth. That is the biblical prospect, the reality which it envisages. The life of heaven and the life of earth will be drawn together in a single new reality, for which the most common biblical description is 'a new heaven and a new earth'.

The importance for the present

Why do we have to think about all this now? We have enough issues to face in the present without anticipating what the future will hold. For many of us, our relationships, our studies, our work or simply making sure the bills are paid gives us quite enough to think about. We are involved warmly and enthusiastically in our churches, perhaps in Christian service. Do we need to think about the future? The answer is all to do with purposefulness.

Creatures with a purpose

How you prepare yourself when you set out on a journey depends to a certain extent on what your destination is going to be like. If we head for the sun, for our summer holidays, we may think about buying some lightweight clothes or a new camera or some suntan oil. We make preparation. Why? Because there is a purpose involved and an end in sight. This says something biblical and profound about our humanness. In this, as in some other important respects, we are distinctively different from the animals with whom we share so many biological similarities: we have a teleological nature—we are creatures with a purpose.

I vividly remember that when I was an undergraduate, before I became a Christian, I was immensely concerned about the question of purpose. Many of us ask, 'What is it all about?' At that time—when I was a musician and an active composer—my answer to that question was divided. I did not believe in God, but I was aware that through music and the arts generally one could perceive something beautiful and purposeful at the heart of things. Yet the philosophy which I read at university told me another story. The French existentialist left-wing philosopher Jean Paul Sartre, was particularly influential in the early seventies. And what he said about purpose stuck fast in my mind. He said: 'It was meaningless that I was born, it is meaningless that I live, and it will be meaningless when I die.' How do we resolve that? Our heart tells us one thing, our head tells us another.

The biblical teaching on the new heaven and new earth provides the answer to that heart-head dilemma. Jesus has done everything for us. One of the things he has done is to create an eternal home for us—it will not be a rest-home, it will be a place of activity. The fact that he has done this lends ultimate meaning to our lives. We are going somewhere; we have a destiny—a teleological purpose—and this affects the sense of purpose which we have in the present. We all have some sense of purpose when things are going well. It is when we come up against obstacles like pain and loss and suffering that our sense of purpose gets knocked off centre. Paul gives us a reminder which will put us back on the right course: 'I consider that the sufferings of this present time are not worth comparing with the glory that is to be revealed to us' (Rom 8:18). For him, the coming 'glory' was obviously a significant perspective-changer.

Glorious things of thee are spoken

Do you keep a stock of glorious moments—the secular as well as the spiritual? If you like Sibelius, it might be the end of his fifth symphony. If you like the theatre, it might be the memory of, or a recording of, Gielgud's rendering of the Hamlet soliloquies. If you love the countryside, it might be the wonderful view or a particular sunset. You might even have a favourite brand of special chocolate which is glorious. These human titbits are a tiny little taster of a far, far greater magnificence, for which the Bible's word is glory. Think of anything you consider really marvellous and wonderful, multiply it an infinity of times over, and you begin to approach the quality of what Paul is speaking of as 'the glory to be revealed'.

The glory that is to be revealed to us is from God. True glory is always a reflection of him. So sufferings, however painful they may be, do somehow pale into insignificance when viewed from an eternal perspective and compared with the glory to come. 'Man is born to trouble as surely as sparks fly upwards' (Job 5:7 NIV). With a real sense of the gloriousness of the place and the person for which we are bound, and a sense of purpose inspired by the vision of the coming new world, no matter how tough the obstacles of pain and suffering in the way, we can find a new perspective and encouragement.

There is an important balance to be maintained here. The pain and the awfulness of suffering is in no way minimized or written off by Paul, or any of the other biblical writers for that matter, but real suffering is set in a context which both transforms and redeems it. This is part of the glorious majesty, part of the work of Christ the King: God recognizes the reality of the present fallen world's hard edges—its pains and suffering—but he does more than that, he has acted decisively to remedy the situation. By the incarnation, he has directly experienced the worst the world can offer, but he has gloriously triumphed over it. His victory has a dual aspect. It's decisive, but from our perspective it has a largely promissory dimension: the victory has been won and we can experience that now, but, on the other hand, although the kingdom of God has been inaugurated, what we currently experience is only a glimpse of the glory that will be revealed to us.

In the Creator's image

'The glory and honour of the nations will be brought into [the heavenly city]. Nothing that is impure will ever enter it' (Rev 21:26 NIV).

This is saying something about creativity in the widest sense. We are made in the image of God the Creator. The God who in Genesis 1 affirmed the goodness of the world he has made is not simply going to write off everything that has been glorious and honourable in the history of the world and of mankind. All that has been good and creative in individual lives and all that has been good in the arts and the sciences is going to be there in the new heaven and new earth—or at least there will be a transformation to an even greater glory of all that has been best and good in every aspect of our lives from the least of us to the greatest. 'The glory and honour of the nations will be brought into [the heavenly city].'

So everything matters. Everything we do is, to a greater or lesser extent, significant for eternity. That is what Jesus is saying in the parable of the talents. In the new heaven and the new earth, nothing impure will enter in. We will leave all that behind. But nothing worth while will be wasted.

Is there something which you feel is badly under-appreciated? Do you sometimes even feel that you are unappreciated? The honour and the glory of all peoples, all that is best, big or small, will find its place of appreciation in the new heaven and the new earth. This is why it is important to dwell on these realities now. It lends an extra dimension of purpose to our lives, because everything good matters—right through to eternity.

What is it all going to be like?

The New Testament interest in the things of the new world is not deeply concerned with fine detail. The New Testament emphasis was once somewhat obscurely put to me as 'theological and soteriological, rather than cosmological'. In everyday language, that means there is not much geographical information given about the new heaven and the new earth. There is not much point in speculating about what it will all look like and feel like.

Those who are scientists may like to attempt to predict the physical basis and processes of a renewed and perfected world. The Bible seems to say there will be both continuity and change. The real point, however, is that God will be right at the visible centre of our lives. This will be as the climax of the whole work of salvation.

> I heard a loud voice from the throne saying, 'Behold, the dwelling of God is with men. He will dwell with them, and they shall be his people, and God himself will be with them; he will wipe away every tear from their eyes, and death shall be no more, neither shall there be mourning nor crying nor pain any more, for the former things have passed away.'
>
> (Rev 21:3-4)

What is heaven going to be like? It is going to involve a powerful presence and a positive absence.

The powerful presence

The powerful presence is God himself. He will dwell with his people. In saying what that is going to mean or be like, it is difficult to get much further than that basic statement. It is going to be remarkable, an experience of unending glory.

When Claire and I became engaged, a friend said to me, 'I expect you can't imagine anything more marvellous than spending a lifetime in Claire's company, can you?' I thought then, 'No, you're right.' And I am glad to say he is still right. When two people are in love, all they want to do is spend time in one another's company. It is one of the ways to tell whether you are in love.

If human love can give us such a sense of glory, how much more glorious it will be when we are in the presence of a God who loves us with a love which we can hardly begin to fathom. The love of God in Jesus is so rich and generous and warm and deep, it is in truth the experience of glory itself.

The positive absence

The positive absence means the absence of tears, death, mourning, crying and pain. This is all to do with the fact of God's loving fatherly presence with us. It is deeply moving. In the new world, there will be no more pain. We all shed tears for the suffering that goes on in our world. And suffering is not just something out there, very often it is in our own lives, either in our personal experience, or in the life of someone we care for deeply. Suffering has so many faces: loss of loved ones, long protracted disabling illness or sadnesses of various kinds. And there is inner suffering too: the suffering of psychological, emotional and spiritual pressures. It can involve painful memories, and coming to terms with painful facts about our own lives.

In the new heaven and the new earth there will be no more pain and no more suffering. There is going to be an end to it. It is not that we are going to be anaesthetized to it all, rather it is because we are going to be transformed, and we shall live for ever in the presence of our loving, caring, heavenly Father. That is why Paul is able to say in Romans 8:18, 'I consider that the sufferings of this present time are not worth comparing with the glory that is to be revealed to us.'

If you know that journey's end is in sight, if you know that happiness which awaits you at the other end, it gives you not only courage to keep going but also joy along the way, no matter what your circumstances. Suffering can be transformed by glory.

Journey's end

Paul, when writing to the Thessalonian Christians, is unable to give a timetable for the second coming; instead, he uses picture-language to emphasize its unpredictable occurrence:

> Now, brothers, about times and dates we do not need to write to you, for you know very well that the day of the Lord will come like a thief in the night. While people are saying, 'Peace and safety', destruction will come on them suddenly, as labour pains on a pregnant woman, and they will not escape.
>
> (1 Thess 5:1-3 NIV)

It is eminently understandable in human terms why we should like to know a precise timetable for the end times. When will Jesus return? When will the judgement be? Will life get better or worse before or after he comes? When he does come, will that be an end to life as we know it altogether? If we only had the times mapped out, how much simpler it would all be! Or would it?

Jesus, like Paul, emphasized that the day of the Lord —the Old Testament term of expectation now seen as the return of Christ—would come not only unexpectedly, but that its date is impossible to calculate: 'No-one knows about that day or hour, not even the angels in heaven, nor the Son, but only the Father' (Mt 24:36 NIV).

In the light of both these statements concerning the unexpectedness and incalculability of the second coming, it is odd indeed that some claim Jesus and Paul expected these events to happen during the lifetime of the early disciples. These texts clearly illustrate that they were at pains not to commit themselves to such a timetable, because only God the Father knows the date he has set.

Conversely, such sects as the Jehovah's Witnesses have looked ridiculously red-faced to the outside world, having confidently predicted the end of the world on at least five occasions—for the years 1874, 1914, 1915, 1975 and 1976. Several times it was a case of quick recalculations all round. Even that master of calculation,

John Napier, the inventor of logarithms, managed to get it wrong, calculating the date of Christ's return anytime between 1688 and 1700. Naturally an authority such as his was closely followed and admired. Consequently his commentary on the book of Revelation had quite a vogue, with twenty-three editions and several translations before the world's predicted deadline. After 1700 it did not seem to sell so well!

Timetabling the kingdom

The reason Jesus was reticent about times and seasons is that we, as kingdom people, are meant to remain thoroughly and passionately active on the King's behalf right up to the moment he returns. We can give him no better welcome that that. It is designed to keep us on our toes. Timetabling the kingdom will inevitably affect in some way our quality, style and intensity of performance on the King's behalf. None the less, for many years Christians of the finest credentials have taken on the task of glimpsing behind the scenes, and have come up with some fascinating observations. The discussion largely revolves around the understanding of Revelation 20, where John describes a period of a thousand years, a time when Satan is bound, preventing him from deceiving the nations any longer. At the end of that thousand year period, Satan is released. Having deceived the nations once more, this time for a short period, he is finally defeated. Thereafter follows the judgement and the new heaven and new earth. The period of a thousand years is referred to as the millennium, and there are four main views as to what it means.

What's in a thousand years?

Premillennialists see Jesus' return as preceding this thousand year period. It bases this view on a strictly chronological appraisal of the arrangement of the book of Revelation. Since Revelation 19 describes the second coming of Christ, it would appear obvious that Revelation 20 describes a thousand year period after that event.

But is Revelation a strict sequence of historical events? There are three sets of visions—the seven seals (6:1-8:5), the seven trumpets (8:6 - 11:19) and the seven bowls (15:1 - 16:21). The most natural reading of them is that they are indeed historical events, but looked at from different standpoints. The three groups are parallel accounts of the same period. Each time, the writer backtracks, adds another layer of colour and changes the perspectives from which the events are viewed. Premillennialists see the world in decay, with Jesus returning after a period of tremendous turmoil and suffering such as is described in Mark 13 and 2 Thessalonians 2. During the thousand-year rule which follows, Christ's power will be finally and fully asserted on earth.

Postmillennialists, as the term suggests, see Jesus returning after the millennium. It is tremendously optimistic, seeing the present age as giving way to Christ's thousand-year rule of triumph through his people.

Amillennialism rejects belief in a future literal thousand-year rule. It sees Revelation 20 as a picture of this present age, with Satan bound and no longer able to deceive the nations, with the gospel enabled to spread, according to the promise to Abraham, to all peoples. The people of God enjoy the present reign of Christ with the powers of the kingdom already revealed, yet wait for the consummation of things with the actual historical coming of Christ at his second coming.

Dispensationalists take a scheme of the future which was largely unknown until J.N. Darby of the Plymouth Brethren movement popularized it in the nineteenth century. The approach of the seven different dispensations in the way God deals with man—innocence, conscience, human government (commencing with Noah), promise, law (from Moses to Christ), grace (the age of the church) and kingdom (the millennium)—and the sequence of eight covenants which, according to *The Scofield Reference Bible*, accompanies it, appears to be a careful and reverent handling of Scripture. However, it implies that God treats men and women in different ways in different periods, and does violence to Scripture's own view of itself as a unity and a witness to the one unfolding plan of salvation.

All four views have this in common: they are anxious for the concerns of Christ and the coming of his kingdom. Premillennialists and postmillennialists have high expectations of what Christ can and will achieve on this earth. They share a strong and vital view of the strength and power of Jesus. Yet premillennialism, committed as it is to a vision of steep decline before the return of Jesus, can lack grit and resolve in social responsibility. Likewise, postmillennialism can appear over-optimistic concerning what can be achieved before Christ's return. Amillennialism seems to many to be the most exegetically accurate position, though it too may have drawbacks of its own.

Christians are bound to differ; although we are all subject to Scripture, our minds are fallen, so none of us has a monopoly on truth and our interpretation of specific scriptures can be at considerable variance. We have to decide on what are primary and what are secondary issues of faith. In the end, theologically, although it has many implications, the millennium is a secondary issue. The reason is clear. Jesus declined to give us a timetable. We should therefore be circumspect and discreet in our pronouncements. One thing is absolutely certain, none of us can evade our responsibility to live in the light of this momentous event, whatever be the day or hour of its coming.

In the light of the future, how should we live in the present?

In 2 Peter 3:14, speaking of the new heaven and the new earth, Peter says, 'Since you wait for these, be zealous to be found by [God] without spot or blemish, and at peace.'

We need to relate this hope and expectation for the future to our present situation. There is a terrible potential for destruction in our world today. The good news of Jesus is that the forgiveness of his cross and the re-creative power of God through the Holy Spirit can restore a measure of order, meaning, freedom, dignity and responsibility to a world which desperately needs hope.

We have to learn to relate our hope for the culmination of history, the return of Jesus and the new world which he will inaugurate to our concrete duties within history now. There are several ways in which the purpose and motive of the new world spur us on.

We are spurred on to evangelism because the new world will contain multitudes from all the nations. We have an important part to play in taking that gospel to all peoples.

We are spurred on to social action because the new world will be a place where righteousness dwells. If right action is to be the primary characteristic of the kingdom to come, then we must work out our duties in this present manifestation of the kingdom.

We are spurred on to love life. The references in Revelation and Isaiah to the wealth and the honour of the nations, teach us to be richly involved with all that is best in the arts and sciences.

We are spurred on to love peace. If, in the new world, as both Isaiah and Micah say, 'they shall beat their swords into ploughshares, and their spears into pruning hooks . . . neither shall they learn war any more' (Is 2:4; Mic 4:3), does that not mean we should pursue peace and aim to be peacemakers in every possible way? 'Every possible way' will include personal relationships at home, at work, in church, in society and internationally.

The prospect of a new heaven and a new earth is an immense encouragement to us, providing us now with real purpose—leading one day to real glory. But there is also an immense challenge to us. It is a challenge which, as kingdom people, people destined to share in the new order, we can in no way evade. That challenge involves the interrelationship between belief and behaviour. It means making the kingdom visible through our lives as we wait for the grand comsummation of all things.

Live in awe

A certain kind of understanding about God, the kingdom, and the final outcome of history, should inspire a certain kind of lifestyle. This is all the more important when it is considered that the issue of belief and behaviour is, sadly, one where Christians all over the world are at their weakest.

It is where the crack shows most clearly: there is a tendency for a gap to open up between belief and behaviour. The way we live so often denies in practice what we believe in theory. And unfortunately, in these situations, the critics of Christianity have a field-day. It is not just the media who observe and comment, it is the people closest to us; they are the ones who watch us. The people in our office or work place, the non-Christians at home, those of our friends who are not Christians—they are all watching us. They may well want to know if there is something in what we believe and what we say we stand for. But we can be sure about one fact. They can smell a phoney a mile off. And it is our responsibility to close up that gap between behaviour and belief, and to bring integrity of lifestyle to what we proclaim about Christ and our commitment to him. Our witness to the good news of the kingdom depends on it.

Diagnosis

The writer to the Hebrews shows that the Jewish Christians of the first century were just as guilty as we are of hypocritical, sub-standard Christian living. By consequence, their witness—like ours—was becoming tame, eroded and ineffective. But the writer makes his diagnosis not upon the basis of their laziness or apathy first of all (though such attitudes were involved); instead, he sees the major failing as to do with something far deeper.

Myopic sight. The major failing is to do with a blunted vision of God, a way of seeing God which does far less than justice to the full truth about him. It is failing to live in awe. And if our sense of the awe of God diminishes, so too will our sense of inspiration to serve him. It is our vision of God, our sense of awe—which includes our love, our gratitude, but also our sense of his surpassing greatness, his majesty and his splendour—which makes the tie-up between behaviour and belief and radically affects our witness.

The writer to the Hebrews urges us, 'Let us offer to God acceptable worship, with reverence and awe; for our God is a consuming fire' (Heb 12:28-29). The worship referred to there, as the context makes clear, is to do with lifestyle, the way we live before God. The New Testament often used the word 'worship' in this wider sense. It does not refer here to the singing of hymns or a church service. It is making the strong point that the whole of our lives are of interest to God, that everything we are, and everything we do, can and should be part of our worship.

Our God 'is a consuming fire', so we must offer to him acceptable worship, with reverence and awe. Is this the way we would normally choose to describe God? Why does the writer use such vivid language as this? What impact is it meant to make upon us? To say our God is a consuming fire is a very strong description. We should ask why. But in order to answer this, we need to go further into the teaching in Hebrews 12.

Three responsibilities

Responsibility for yourself. It is easy to become despondent especially when things do not go our own way. We hardly need reminding of that, because it is so obvious. But the danger with despondency is that it can produce inertia within us. And when inertia sets in, we can begin to lose our direction, our energy and our sense of purpose.

Even when the things which go wrong in our lives are small and relatively trivial, it is easy to end up feeling so tired and despondent that you want to pack up and do precisely nothing. Most of us feel like this from time to time. Inertia sets in and we feel sorry for ourselves, even if it is all fairly inconsequential. If we let them, our emotions do exert a very powerful influence over us.

The real danger with despondency is that it brings with it this eroding aspect of inertia. It saps our vision of God and his purposes for us. We look inwards instead of outwards and upwards, and gradually we grind slowly to a halt. The enthusiasm, inspiration and zeal we have had all comes to an end. It is more than feeling sorry for ourselves. When inertia sets in, we become ineffective at the very point where there is most potential for growth.

Whether our troubles are relatively trivial and slight, or whether they are deeply disquieting and a tremendous burden to us, the danger of despondency is the same. It leads to inertia. And it is precisely to those who are going through this experience of despondency, that these words in Hebrews 12 are addressed: 'Therefore lift your drooping hands and strengthen your weak knees, and make straight paths for your feet, so that what is lame may not be put out of joint but rather be healed' (Heb 12:12-13).

Every problem, difficulty and struggle for us as Christians, carries within it the potential for growth; what is lame can be put out of joint, but alternatively it can be healed. So we have to guard against despondency. Whether our troubles be light or burdensome, none of us is ever going to be immune from trouble of one kind or another. We cannot avoid it. We have to learn to face it and accept it. As the first part of Hebrews 12 suggests, God permits such things not to hurt us, but to aid us in our growth in maturity as his children.

The first responsibility is for ourselves: not to sink into despondency, and its consequence of inertia, but to keep our vision clear, and our commitment strong.

Responsibility for our relationships. It is fascinating that attention is now immediately drawn to the question of relationships. It is in our relationships where we discover the most upsetting conflicts we are liable to experience in life. Sadly, in our stupidity, we contribute liberally to those conflicts only too often. We have to take seriously our responsibility in relationships. We are to 'strive for peace with all men, and for the holiness without which no one will see the Lord' (Heb 12:14). In the

Greek, the word for 'strive' is a very strong expression. Notice too that there is an important theological link between peace and holiness. Holiness means becoming more like God. It implies committing ourselves to his will, to his ways of doing things. It is desiring to become more like Christ. How then do holiness and peace link up, especially in relationships?

Picture a problem in a relationship of some kind. Imagine there is someone who continually annoys you; it might be somebody in the family or somebody with whom you work, but whoever they are, it is someone who goads you, or whose attitudes or actions are to you like a red rag to a bull—they make you boil.

What can you do about it? You have tried, but the arguments or the anger within continually get the better of you. You tried and you failed . . . and failed . . . and failed again. It is dispiriting. It can make you despondent. Worse still, inertia can set in, then we simply learn, through continuing discouragement, to accept the aggravation as a normal part of our life. There must be an alternative. What is the way forward?

The clue is the link between peace and holiness which the writer to the Hebrews highlights. When we strive for holiness in our lives, bringing our lives into willing conformity with God's purposes, then a practical way of peace is so much more possible for us.

One cause of conflict between us has to do with our sensitivities. We all know that under the surface of our lives there lurk all kinds of personal sensitivities. They are the emotional baggage of our lives which we have been carrying around with us since our childhood. We are all of us very sensitive underneath the surface. The problem comes when someone steps on one of our most cherished inner pains.

This happens when those inner sensitivities become threatened. They become threatened by someone else's words or actions, or simply by what they stand for, or even by association with the memory of words, attitudes or actions of things now past. What happens is we rush to the defence of our sensitive inner selves. We wave our own words around like offensive weapons, and then the sparks fly upwards. Acrimony is the order of the day. No one is immune. As Christians, how can we counteract this weakness within ourselves?

There is a way forward, and it is to do with holiness. When we give up our lives to Christ, and more and more seek for holiness, we give God a chance to heal these inner sensitivities of ours by actually letting him into our bruised inner selves. It is like removing a plaster, exposing a wound to the fresh air and letting it heal in the open. It is something we must do. We must open our lives fully to God, and let him touch the painful parts of our lives: the parts where there is resentment and hurt, the areas where there is a real need for change on our part. The points at which change is required may have to do with our attitudes and our expectations, or they may relate to our need fully and unreservedly to forgive another person.

Our relationships matter, especially those relationships with people who have wronged us. We need to put right the attitudes within ourselves. We cannot nurse anger for ever. It will get the better of us in the end. Jesus' forgiveness enables us to forgive those who have hurt or wronged us. As Christians we are being scrutinized; people do look to the way we handle our relationships, and it is there that they may question whether Christianity works or not. It is as basic as that. This is the way to live and please God; it is the way others show the powerful reality of Christ's kingdom and the new world to which we are called.

Knowledge of this equation between peace and holiness is important. Furthermore, we can point to another principle: the quality of our relationships with each other is dependent on our relationship with God. If holiness comes first you will be enabled to pursue the way of peace in your dealings with others. Neglect God and his righteousness and your relationships suffer. Holiness keeps us on course. It enables us to work at peace in our relationships. It liberates us inwardly, because we are making room for God in our lives.

Responsibility for others. We have a responsibility for one another. The overall concern of Jesus when he spoke of his second coming was that his subjects should be ready for him when he comes. We do have to close the gap between behaviour and belief. And we have a responsibility for each other, to help one another know the grace of God in our lives: 'See to it that no one fail to obtain the grace of God; that no "root of bitterness" spring up and cause trouble, and by it the many become defiled; that no one be immoral or irreligious like Esau' (Heb 12:15-16). This is the wider responsibility: we are not just to be concerned for the specific relationships we have at home, work and in our general social friendships, we must also recognize our general responsibility towards all Christians, and especially the members of the churches of which we are members.

There used to be an awful Christian syndrome. It went something like this. You would bump into another Christian at church. You smiled broadly, then out came the conditional reflex: 'How are you?' 'Fine!' was the sometimes less than honest reply. And one goofy grin later, off you both went again, happily singing your respective choruses under your breath, your lives not having touched.

The excesses of sincerity can be just as bad.

'How *are* you?' (The eyes are fixed to yours.)

'Er, very well thank you.'

'But how are you *really*?'

They are both just caricatures. But unfortunately in any social situation, and especially in churches, extremes are always dangerously present. They range between shallow insincerity or nosy paternalism.

How much do you care about other people in your church? How much do you care about other Christians in your place of work or study? Do you care at all? Are you concerned about how other Christians are doing? Whether they are under pressure, struggling, discouraged or despondent, it is our role to encourage other Christians. But we will not do this by hearty slaps on the back. For us as Christians encouragement comes in two ways: by love and by prayer.

In order to love a person you have to give time to them. You cannot love without time spent. Love is far more than a feeling. To express love requires the expenditure of time. So we must not skimp on the time we spend with people. We all need encouraging spiritually. We all need to be listened to. We all of us need to be loved. Sadly it is possible to be charging around, spreading ourselves as thin as can be, not really allowing ourselves time to connect in a real way with each other's lives.

We have three responsibilities: to ourselves, to our relationships, and to other Christians—especially those within our local church. Neglect any of them, and the crack begins to open up between behaviour and belief. We have to beware of the sin of diversification. Don't do too much. Don't become too busy. Don't spread yourself too thin. If you do, what happens next proceeds inevitably and predictably. First you will suffer. Then your relationships will suffer. And then the church will suffer. For the world to see the changed lives which Jesus Christ makes possible, we need to work at all three responsibilities—we cannot afford to let them slip.

The two worlds

We often speak about someone being highly motivated, goal-orientated and having real direction in life. It makes all the difference in the end. When I was a music student, I used to be fascinated by the piano writing of Franz Liszt. Liszt was the greatest piano virtuoso of the nineteenth century—in fact probably of all time. And his piano writing, particularly the transcendental études, is the most ingenious, creative, virtuosic and technically demanding work for the piano in the whole of the literature. It is stupendous.

Liszt was one of the most goal-orientated artists of the nineteenth century. He was a pupil of Karl Czerny, the man who wrote all the five-finger exercises. Czerny himself had been a pupil of Beethoven. One day the young

Franz Liszt heard the legendary violinist Paganini. Paganini was so extraordinarily remarkable as a violinist, that people used to say he was in league with the devil. He was a phenomenon. Again, there has never been a virtuoso like him.

Liszt was so bowled over by Paganini's playing, he resolved there and then to turn his back on the past, the world of Beethoven and Czerny, and to re-create on the piano the fantastic virtuosity and ingenuity and brilliance that Paganini had displayed on the violin. He worked at it all his life. The remarkable transcendental études were the result. They are truly staggering. Liszt knew what he wanted to do. He had his goals set out. He knew where he was going.

In a spiritual sense, we need to have our goals mapped out too. We need to know where we are going. Hebrews 12 describes and illustrates two possible worlds one could work towards. One is the past; the other is the future.

The world of the past is verses 18 to 21. It is the world of Moses and the giving of the law. The Hebrew Christians were harking back all the time. But the past is not relevant, certainly not in terms of goals—nor as something to work towards. Our motivation can never be the past. It must always be the future.

The point here is that the Hebrew Christians did not have any goals mapped out. They did not have that sense of working towards a future which is entirely in the purposes of God. That, by contrast, is the point of verses 22 to 24: 'You have come to Mount Zion and to the city of the living God . . .' We have been incorporated into God's kingdom, we are part of his people, and we are working towards a goal. Lose sight of the goal, and you immediately loosen the relationship between belief and behaviour. Those three responsibilities of self, relationships and others do not matter so much if you have nothing to work towards and there is no future seriously to consider.

So which world are you working towards? Are you taking the risks of faith which are a necessary part of working towards the future with God? Or are you more preoccupied with the past? Our priorities need a regular check-up. Again, if you let yourself get too busy, your vision can get stifled.

One consequence

'Thus let us offer to God acceptable worship, with reverence and awe; for our God is a consuming fire' (Heb 12:28-29).

Fire in Scripture is often a visual aid which illustrates God's holiness; think, for instance, of the fire of the burning bush, or the fire of Sinai. What is your vision of God? Do you have before your mind the blazing heat of God's holiness, his justice, his righteousness and his love? He burns so much with care for us that he sent Jesus Christ to die so we could become his children. Do you realize it is this God, the consuming fire, whose child you are? This God cares passionately about you, about the way you live, about the way you contribute to his kingdom; he cares about the way you treat yourself, about your relationships and about other Christians.

Our God *is* a consuming fire. He burns with ferocious anger when that crack opens up between behaviour and belief, because it means we have lost our vision of God, of the future and of our part in it.

There are three responsibilities, two worlds and one consequence. 'Thus let us offer to God acceptable worship, with reverence and with awe.' Why? Because we are God's kingdom people. The God who reigns has acted out of love and mercy to bring us into an everlasting covenant relationship with himself. Our responsibility is to live for his glory; that means sowing the seed of the word, which itself depends on the integrity of our witness to the King by the discharge of our kingdom responsibilities with the same passion for justice and mercy as the King himself. Effective communication of the gospel of the kingdom depends on this. We are called to be holy, to reflect the holiness of the God who loves us. It means that, as a kingdom people, we are called out to be *different*.

What part are you playing in that difference? Is it true of you? Go back to your vision of God. We need to live in awe. Our friends, our families, those we work with all watch us. They can smell a phoney a mile off. Have you a blunted vision of God? Our God is a consuming fire. For the sake of the purposes of the kingdom which is unfolding with glory, whose full reality is soon to be consummated, we are under an obligation. As we move towards the future, before a watching world, we are the heralds of the kingdom of God. We must, therefore, narrow the gap between behaviour and belief.

For the unfolding kingdom to touch the lives of our generation and any generations which remain, we must be the King's faithful witnesses. The question is as pointed today as when it was first addressed to the disciples (Lk 18:8): When the Son of Man comes—when Jesus the King returns to usher in the fullness of the kingdom—*will he find faith on the earth?*